Green Finance and Investment

Accessing and Using Green Finance in the Kyrgyz Republic

EVIDENCE FROM A HOUSEHOLD SURVEY

OECD

BETTER POLICIES FOR BETTER LIVES

This work is published under the responsibility of the Secretary-General of the OECD. The opinions expressed and arguments employed herein do not necessarily reflect the official views of OECD member countries.

This document, as well as any data and map included herein, are without prejudice to the status of or sovereignty over any territory, to the delimitation of international frontiers and boundaries and to the name of any territory, city or area.

Please cite this publication as:
OECD (2021), *Accessing and Using Green Finance in the Kyrgyz Republic: Evidence from a Household Survey*, Green Finance and Investment, OECD Publishing, Paris, *https://doi.org/10.1787/6233a44f-en*.

ISBN 978-92-64-61524-3 (print)
ISBN 978-92-64-37078-4 (pdf)

Green Finance and Investment
ISSN 2409-0336 (print)
ISSN 2409-0344 (online)

Foreword

The National Bank of the Kyrgyz Republic expressed interest in working with the Organisation for Economic Co-operation and Development (OECD) on an analysis of household savings and investment behaviour. Ultimately, it wanted this analysis to help the Kyrgyz banking sector embed climate change into financial decisions and macroeconomic analysis. The bank monitors several indicators of financial sector breadth such as branch, automated teller machines and deposit penetration. Savings behaviour and the particular demands of the Kyrgyz population for financial products and services, however, are still little understood.

This report presents findings from a survey conducted among 1 000 households in the Kyrgyz Republic in 2019. The research aimed to identify needs and demand from potential and existing clients of Kyrgyz financial institutions for financial instruments and solutions to promote sustainable development. The study results will be used to help implement the National Sustainable Development Strategy of the Kyrgyz Republic 2018-2040 and help inform the main directions of the banking system and medium-term strategies for 2022-2025.

Isabella Neuweg (OECD) wrote this report and interpreted the survey results. Takayoshi Kato (OECD) conceptualised and helped design the household survey. Krzysztof Michalak (OECD) provided overall guidance. The household survey was carried out by SIAR Research and Consulting. The author would like to thank in particular the National Bank of the Kyrgyz Republic and especially Bakyt Tynaliev and Zhyldyz Sulaimanbekova for their continuous support in the implementation of this project, as well as their intellectual contributions. The author would like to thank Maya Lalieva for her comments on Chapter 2 and for her help during project implementation. The author is also grateful to Luiza Mamarasulova from the International Finance Corporation for her expert review of the report and her helpful insights. The author thanks Elnura Ibraeva for her continuous support and her professionalism throughout the study and Ainoura Sagynbaeva for her feedback on the report (both SIAR Research and Consulting). The author also thanks the Union of Banks of Kyrgyzstan for highlighting their work on sustainable finance. The report greatly benefited from expert reviews and valuable suggestions from colleagues at the OECD Secretariat that have made the report more focused, clearer and more readable: Krzysztof Michalak, Cecilia Tam, David Simek, Jean-Francois Lengelle, Mikaela Rambali and Guy Halpern. The author is grateful to conference participants at the Sixth Annual Life in Kyrgyzstan Conference 2020 for their comments and to the conference organisers for the opportunity to present the study. The author is very thankful to Maria Dubois, Mark Foss, Lupita Johanson and Jonathan Wright for editing assistance.

This work was financially supported by the German Federal Ministry for the Environment, Nature Conservation and Nuclear Safety, and implemented under the GREEN Action Task Force hosted by the OECD.

Table of contents

Tables

Figures

List of acronyms and abbreviations

ASEAN	Association of Southeast Asian Nations
ATM	automated teller machine
EBRD	European Bank for Reconstruction and Development
ERIA	Economic Research Institute for ASEAN and East Asia
ESG	environment, social and governance
GDP	gross domestic product
IFC	International Finance Corporation
ILO	International Labour Organization
Ishenim CJSC	Ishenim Credit Bureau
KGS	Kyrgyz som
OECD	Organisation for Economic Co-operation and Development
PAGE	Partnership for Action on Green Economy
SMEs	small and medium-sized enterprises
UNDP	United Nations Development Programme
UNICEF	United Nations Children's Fund
USD	US Dollar

Executive summary

The government of the Kyrgyz Republic (Kyrgyzstan) needs structural reforms to strengthen macroeconomic performance, reduce poverty and address challenges posed by human-made climate change. In recognition of these challenges, the government has set out the National Sustainable Development Strategy towards 2040. In addition, it has launched the Green Economy Program 2019-2023, which guides its transition towards an economy that is green and inclusive. Managing the COVID-19 pandemic and its consequences presents the opportunity to accelerate this transition and embed principles to implement it into short and medium-term economic planning.

The banking sector can improve the fiscal base for structural reforms towards the green, inclusive transition by bringing flows of money from the informal economy (making up almost one-fourth of gross domestic product) into official channels. It can also mobilise additional green investments. However, deeper understanding is required on two levels to explore the potential of the Kyrgyz banking system to help mobilise such finance. First, on the supply side, more knowledge is needed on the functions and efficacy of the banking system and financial regulations. Second, on the demand side, more insight is required in areas such as the needs of individuals, households, entrepreneurs and businesses for financial solutions that support the transition to a green and inclusive economy. The study presented here focuses on the demand side.

This report uses household-level data collected through a survey of 1 000 households in the Kyrgyz Republic in the summer of 2019 to analyse access to, as well as use and perceptions of, green finance. In the context of the survey, green finance is defined as a household's investments to reduce its emissions, improve energy efficiency, reduce water consumption, improve forestry management, protect biodiversity or improve climate resilience.

Responses to the household survey show that:

- 30% of households had taken out a loan or credit to finance one or several activities with a climate mitigation or adaptation purpose in the past five years.
- 40% did not know whether they had taken out a loan or credit to finance any of these activities, which points to a lack of understanding of green finance; 70% did not know whether they were interested in doing so in the near future.
- use of formal financial services in general was low (more than 80% of respondents did not have a bank account).

The survey points to a clear gap in knowledge and understanding of the pros and cons of green investment and that many respondents had not previously reflected on making green investments. Respondents perceived high interest rates as the biggest barrier to taking out a green loan. Short lending terms, insufficient collateral, inconvenient repayment schedules were additional barriers. Respondents also think their insufficient knowledge on how to access and use banking services would hinder them from taking out a green loan. Other barriers noted include lack of bank accounts, lack of information on banking products and insufficient information on the purpose of green financial products.

The results highlight the need to increase general financial literacy, access to bank accounts, and understanding and awareness of green financial products.

The report identifies three main pathways for better access to and use of green financial products:

1. Strengthening the regulatory requirements for financial institutions, e.g. by making it mandatory for financial providers to improve environmental, social and governance principles in their operations.

2. Broadening and better targeting financial products to the needs of Kyrgyz households. This can include providing financial incentives for agricultural and disaster risk insurance, promoting movable asset-based lending or helping customers combine remittance accounts with other financial products.

3. Improving financial literacy on green financial products and services, among both households and financial service providers.

Overall, the survey highlights that improving access to and use of green financial products and services needs to go hand in hand with efforts to increase use of formal financial instruments. A functioning financial market where households and businesses actively use financial products and services is in many ways a precondition for introducing elements of green finance. A comprehensive regulatory and financial framework that tackles financial inclusion, social inclusion and green finance together will help implement mutually reinforcing policy actions; create synergies between economic, social and environmental goals; and achieve progress faster.

1 Background and relevance of the study

This chapter outlines the background to the OECD's study and the household survey. It describes how the National Bank of the Kyrgyz Republic expressed interest in working with the OECD to source new evidence on the extent to which households access and use (green) financial products and services. It describes how the Kyrgyz National Sustainable Development Strategy for 2018-2040 and the Green Economy Program contain targets on sustainable finance. Finally, the chapter presents the socio-economic context of the Kyrgyz Republic, and outlines how the banking sector could help the country achieve its sustainable development goals.

Strategies to support green and inclusive development

In 2018, the Kyrgyz Republic adopted the National Sustainable Development Strategy for 2018-2040 and the Development Program of Kyrgyzstan for 2018-2022. The Strategy and the Program commit to implementing and facilitating actions needed for economic development that is green and inclusive. The Ministry of Economy worked with the United Nations Development Programme (UNDP) and other actors under the Partnership for Action on Green Economy (PAGE)[1] to promote greening of the Kyrgyz economy. Together, they developed the Green Economy Program for 2019-2023, which outlines specific actions towards the goal of a green and inclusive transition.

Sustainable finance features prominently in those strategies and programme as a core means to implement green policy priorities in sectors such as energy, farming, industry and transport. Green finance or sustainable finance (used interchangeably in this report) refer to monetary flows into climate adaptation or climate mitigation activities. The steps in promoting sustainable finance in the Green Economy Program include the following:

- Identify the potential demand and needs of the banking sector to implement the principles of Green Finance.
- Prepare the banking and microfinance sectors for the International Finance Corporation Preparedness Standard.
- Implement systems for assessing, monitoring, controlling and supporting green economy activities of financial institutions.
- Train employees and customers of Kyrgyz commercial banks and microfinance institutions.
- Implement sustainable financing in the banking and microfinance sector.
- Explore a potential mechanism for Green Finance.

The National Bank of the Kyrgyz Republic expressed interest to work with the OECD on a detailed diagnostic study that would help implement the country's Green Economy Program. This report presents findings from a household survey that explores aspects related to the demand side of the financial system. The research sought to identify needs and demand from potential and existing clients of Kyrgyz financial institutions for financial instruments and solutions to promote activities contributing to sustainable development. The study results will be used to implement the National Sustainable Development Strategy of the Kyrgyz Republic 2018-2040 and help inform the main directions of the banking system and medium-term strategy documents for 2022-2025.

The Kyrgyz context

The Kyrgyz Republic (Kyrgyzstan) is a lower middle-income country with a small, open economy reliant on trade partners, notably the People's Republic of China, the Russian Federation (hereafter "Russia") and Kazakhstan (World Bank Group, 2020[1]; EIU Country Analysis, 2020[2]). Exports, especially gold, and household spending were the main drivers of economic growth in 2018 and 2019. This resulted in an increase of real gross domestic product (GDP) by 4.5% year on year in 2019 (EIU Country Analysis, 2019[3]; EIU Country Analysis, 2020[2]). The gold mine Kumtor contributes around 10% of GDP (World Bank Group, 2020[1]). Remittances, i.e. direct financial or in-kind transfers to families or communities from people who have migrated abroad to work (OECD, 2019[4]), account for more than 30% of GDP (EIU Country Analysis, 2020[2]). Most Kyrgyz migrant workers are employed in Russia (EIU Country Analysis, 2020[2]).

Kyrgyzstan remains vulnerable to cyclical macroeconomic factors. These include changes in gold prices and a downturn in its major trade partners due to its dependence on gold exports and reliance on remittances (EIU Country Analysis, 2020[2]). The Kyrgyz banking sector would be indirectly impacted if macroeconomic changes or currency risks negatively impact the financial performance of banking sector clients. A highly volatile national currency exchange rate, for example, could worsen the financial condition of borrowers of service loans in foreign currency. Movements in the Russian rouble also impact the Kyrgyz currency, Kyrgyz som (KGS), as Russia is a leading trade partner and a major source of remittance inflows (EIU Country Analysis, 2020[2]).

The som was expected to be relatively stable in 2020/21 (EIU Country Analysis, 2020[2]) and the banking sector expected to withstand macroeconomic shocks (National Bank of the Kyrgyz Republic, 2018[5]). The consequences of the COVID-19 pandemic, however, have led to a decrease of the som against the US dollar (USD) in March 2020. They have also opened a balance of payments gap estimated at USD 400 million (around KGS 30 billion[2]); international financial institutions have released funds to support the Kyrgyz state budget (Reuters, 2020[6]).

GDP per head (in purchasing-power-parity terms) stood at USD 4 000 in 2018 (compared with USD 27 458 for Kazakhstan) (EIU Country Analysis, 2020[2]). According to UNICEF (2016[7]), around 40% of children were living in poverty in the Kyrgyz Republic in 2015. This means they have poor access to quality social services and protection, miss out on education and health care, and face malnutrition. Nearly all of the country is vulnerable to frequent earthquakes, avalanches, floods, mudflows and landslides (UNICEF, 2016[7]). The impacts of climate change will likely exacerbate the situation without preventative measures and investments (UNICEF, 2016[7]). The Kyrgyz government is increasingly prioritising social support measures to reduce poverty as part of its National Sustainable Development Strategy for 2018-2040 (UNICEF, 2016[7]; Government of the Kyrgyz Republic, 2018[8]).

Electricity tariffs are one of the lowest in the world. This leads to underinvestment in existing and new assets, unreliable supply and one of the highest energy intensities in the region (Holzhacker and Skakova, 2019[9]). All of the Kyrgyz population has access to electricity (World Bank, 2020[10]). However, quality and reliability of the electricity supply are much lower compared to other countries in the region and remain issues that need to be tackled (World Bank, 2017[11]). This is especially the case during the winter when the risk of network failure is highest due to increased demand (World Bank, 2017[11]).

Greater quality and reliability of electricity would ensure that households and businesses have undisrupted access to electricity and heat. Reliable heat and electricity supply increases the comfort and health of people and guarantees that businesses can operate smoothly. The Kyrgyz government can also do more to harness sources of hydropower, such as its rivers, to allow for electricity exports since the country uses less than 1% of its renewable energy potential (Holzhacker and Skakova, 2019[9]).

Cleaner sources of electricity and heat would also prevent people from dying of, or living with, the consequences of respiratory illnesses in those households not connected to the grid or district heating (World Bank, 2020[12]). Indeed, 90% of these households use solid fuels such as coal, dung or wood. This increases their exposure to ambient and indoor air pollution, which in turn substantially increases their risk of lung diseases (Gordon et al., 2014[13]; Cragg, Williams and Chavannes, 2016[14]; World Bank, 2020[12]). Substantive reforms of the electricity sector are needed to unlock the large financial resources required to invest in new low-carbon energy sources, power and electricity grids, as well as energy efficiency. The returns would come in the form of increased productivity of businesses and people, and improved health and well-being.

State capacity remains weak, however, to carry out structural reforms and corruption is pervasive (EIU Country Analysis, 2020[2]). The large shadow economy, estimated to make up almost 25% of GDP (National Statistical Committee of the Kyrgyz Republic, 2020[15]), and low administrative capacities make it difficult to collect taxes (EIU Country Analysis, 2019[3]). The government needs an adequate fiscal base to carry out economic reforms; to provide public goods to increase the standard of living and well-being; and to employ well-trained officials. One priority of the government will therefore be to improve tax collectability. The banking sector can play a role here by bringing informal flows of money into official channels. This sector can also help mobilise additional finance for green investments. To that end, it could develop green financial products and services, invest in capabilities and infrastructure to deliver them, scale up green finance practices, aggregate demand for green finance and measure progress.

References

Cragg, L., S. Williams and N. Chavannes (2016), "FRESH AIR: An implementation research project funded through Horizon 2020 exploring the prevention, diagnosis and treatment of chronic respiratory diseases in low-resource settings", *NPJ Primary Care Respiratory Medicine*, Vol. 26/16035, http://dx.doi.org/10.1038/npjpcrm.2016.35. [14]

EIU Country Analysis (2020), *Country Report: Kyrgyz Republic*, The Economist Intelligence Unit, https://store.eiu.com/product/country-report/kyrgyz-republic. [2]

EIU Country Analysis (2019), *Country Report Kyrgyzstan 3rd Quarter*, 11 August, The Economist Intelligence Unit, http://www.alacrastore.com/eiu-economic-data-analysis/Country-Report-Kyrgyzstan-3rd-Quarter-2020-CR_CRKG_MAIN_20200811T000000_0000>. [3]

Gordon, S. et al. (2014), "Respiratory risks from household air pollution in low and middle income countries", *The Lancet Respiratory Medicine*, Vol. 2/10, pp. 823-860, https://doi.org/10.1016/S2213-2600(14)70168-7. [13]

Government of the Kyrgyz Republic (2018), *National Development Strategy of the Kyrgyz Republic for 2018 to 2040*, Government of the Kyrgyz Republic, Bishkek, http://donors.kg/images/National_Development_Strategy_of_KR_2018-2040_final_ENG.docx. [8]

Holzhacker, H. and D. Skakova (2019), *Kyrgyz Republic Diagnostic*, European Bank for Reconstruction and Development, London, https://www.ebrd.com/documents/policy/country-diagnostic-paper-kyrgyz-republic.pdf?blobnocache=true. [9]

National Bank of the Kyrgyz Republic (2018), *The Financial Sector Stability Report of the Kyrgyz Republic, December 2018*, National Bank of the Kyrgyz Republic, Bishkek, https://www.nbkr.kg/DOC/11022019/000000000051647.pdf. [5]

National Statistical Committee of the Kyrgyz Republic (2020), "Unobserved economy in 2018", 24 January, News, National Statistical Committee of the Kyrgyz Republic, Bishkek, http://www.stat.kg/ru/news/nenablyudaemaya-ekonomika-v-2018-godu/. [15]

OECD (2019), *Financial Literacy Needs of Migrants and their Families in the Commonwealth of Independent States*, Paris, http://www.oecd.org/daf/fin/financial-education/financial-education.htm. [4]

Reuters (2020), "IMF approves $120.9 million disbursement for Kyrgyzstan to fight coronavirus", 27 March, Reuters, https://www.reuters.com/article/us-health-coronavirus-imf-kyrgyzstan/imf-approves-1209-million-disbursement-for-kyrgyzstan-to-fight-coronavirus-idUSKBN21E0DN. [6]

UNICEF (2016), *Children in Kyrgyzstan*, webpage, https://www.unicef.org/kyrgyzstan/children-kyrgyzstan (accessed on 24 October 2020). [7]

World Bank (2020), *Access to electricity (% of population) - Kyrgyz Republic*, (database), https://data.worldbank.org/indicator/EG.ELC.ACCS.ZS?locations=KG (accessed on 25 November 2020). [10]

World Bank (2020), *Fueling Kyrgyzstan's Transition to Clean Household Heating Solutions*, World Bank, Washington, DC, http://documents1.worldbank.org/curated/en/164771590727056929/pdf/Fueling-Kyrgyzstan-s-Transition-to-Clean-Household-Heating-Solutions.pdf. [12]

World Bank (2017), "Analysis of the Kyrgyz Republic's Energy Sector", *Working Paper*, No. 122080, World Bank, Washington, DC, http://documents.worldbank.org/curated/en/370411513356783137/Analysis-of-the-Kyrgyz-Republics-Energy-Sector. [11]

World Bank Group (2020), "The World Bank in the Kyrgyz Republic", webpage, https://www.worldbank.org/en/country/kyrgyzrepublic/overview (accessed on 17 April 2020). [1]

Notes

[1] PAGE brings together five UN agencies – UN Environment, International Labour Organization, UN Development Programme, UN Industrial Development Organization and UN Institute for Training and Research – to co-ordinate UN action on green economy and to assist countries in achieving and monitoring the emerging Sustainable Development Goals, especially SDG 8: *"Promote sustained, inclusive and sustainable economic growth, full and productive employment and decent work for all."*

[2] Conversion rate in this report at USD 1 ~ KGS 83, KGS 1 ~ USD 0.012.

2 Banking in the Kyrgyz Republic

This chapter describes the challenges facing the Kyrgyz banking system. It then briefly explains why financial access and use of formal financial instruments are important for economic development. It suggests ways to increase financial access in the Kyrgyz Republic. Several instruments are proposed to improve financial literacy; to provide affordable, targeted financial products by lowering credit risk, alleviating collateral constraints and pooling demand; to increase trust in financial institutions; and to improve access to physical banking infrastructure. Some of these instruments already exist in the country and could be scaled up. Others have worked in countries from the region and beyond, and could be adopted.

Financial development and the Kyrgyz banking sector

As one key area of focus, this report aims to understand the demand for and use of green financial instruments. If there is little use of financial products and services in general, then use of green financial products and services (a subset of financial instruments) will also be limited. Widening access to and use of green financial products and services therefore needs to go hand in hand with development of the financial market in Kyrgyzstan. A functioning financial market where households and businesses actively use financial products and services is in many ways a precondition for introducing elements of green finance.

When compared with other countries in the region, the Kyrgyz Republic's financial development[1] is at par with Tajikistan but lags behind Uzbekistan and Kazakhstan (Yamano et al., 2019[1]). Credit to the private sector as a share of gross domestic product (GDP) has almost doubled since 2011, from about 12% to almost 24% in 2018. However, Kyrgyzstan still ranks low in credit and deposit penetration compared to other countries in the Europe and Central Asia region and compared to other lower middle-income countries (Figure 2.1). Financing is mostly short term and concentrated in a few sectors (trade and agriculture), and the cost of financing remains expensive (Yamano et al., 2019[1]).

Figure 2.1. Domestic credit to private sector by banks (percentage of GDP), in 2018

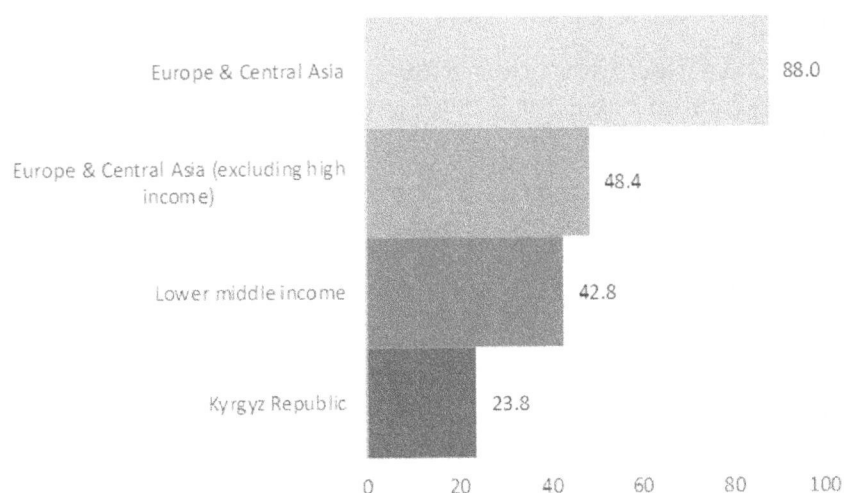

Source: International Monetary Fund, International Financial Statistics; World Bank and OECD GDP estimates, 2020.

In the latest round of World Bank surveys with business owners and top managers in Kyrgyzstan, around 20% of enterprises identified access to finance as a major constraint for business growth (World Bank, 2020[2]).

The survey prepared by the OECD that forms the subject of this report explores in depth the reality for households rather than for businesses. The situation of households, however, mirrors conditions for enterprises in terms of access to and use of financial services in two ways. First, households and entrepreneurs face similar obstacles. Second, household members are often business owners. Almost 420 000 individual entrepreneurs were operating in the Kyrgyz Republic as of October 2020 (compared to 12 000 small and medium-sized enterprises [SMEs]) (National Statistical Committee of the Kyrgyz Republic, 2020[3]). Individual entrepreneurs contribute more than 20% to GDP and their share might be higher given the large informal sector; 60% of agricultural producers are SMEs (Holzhacker and Skakova, 2019[4]). SMEs contribute more than 40% to Kyrgyz GDP. However, their actual contribution is likely higher because of the large informal economy mentioned above and further explained below (Holzhacker and Skakova, 2019[4]).

Commercial banks dominate the banking sector in Kyrgyzstan. As of December 2020, 23 commercial banks and over 300 of their branches operated in the Kyrgyz Republic (National Bank of the Kyrgyz Republic, 2020[5]). Banks account for almost 90% of financial system assets and provide about 80% of credit to the private sector (OECD, 2019[6]). With the exception of microfinance organisations, other financial institutions such as insurance providers, securities and brokerage firms play a marginal role. In addition, capital markets are shallow, including the government securities market (OECD, 2019[6]).

The microfinance sector was established with the help of international donors (OECD, 2018[7]). Half of its credit resources for loans still comes from international donors (OECD, 2019[6]). The number of microfinance organisations has decreased significantly since 2011 (OECD, 2019[6]). This decline followed a period of consolidation, during which the National Bank of the Kyrgyz Republic withdrew licences of over 100 microfinance organisations and a few of them became banks. In September 2020, the sector consisted of slightly over 130 microfinance institutions and around 95 credit unions (National Bank of the Kyrgyz Republic, 2020[8]). Only eight credit unions had a licence to attract deposits in 2016 (National Bank of the Kyrgyz Republic, 2018[9]). Credit unions operate mostly in rural areas and small towns and their lending focuses mainly on agriculture and trade (National Bank of the Kyrgyz Republic, 2018[9]).

Obstacles to greater access to and use of financial products and services

A number of obstacles prevent wider access to and use of financial products and services. These include lack of financial infrastructure, an informal economy, low trust and low financial literacy rates among the population. They are described briefly in turn.

First, due to high poverty rates in Kyrgyzstan, a high proportion of households do not have enough savings to justify a bank account (OECD, 2019[6]). Half of respondents in the 2017 World Bank *Findex* survey in the Kyrgyz Republic gave lack of money as a reason for not having a bank account (Demirgüç-Kunt et al., 2018[10]).

Second, trust in the financial system is low. People, especially the older generation, have lost their savings in the banking crises of the 1990s when several Kyrgyz banks became insolvent (Fitzgeorge-Parker, 2018[11]). Many people prefer to keep their money in traditional ways, i.e. "under the mattress" (OECD, 2019[6]). The *Findex* survey (Demirgüç-Kunt et al., 2018[10]) found that almost a quarter of the Kyrgyz population saved some money, but only 3% of them did so at a financial institution. According to OECD (2019[6]), the population also has limited knowledge about the deposit protection system in the Kyrgyz Republic. Established in 2008, the Deposit Insurance Agency in co-operation with Kyrgyz banks operates a deposit insurance system. This system is mandatory for all commercial banks and protects deposits up to KGS 100 000 in case of a default (Tovar-García and Kozubekova, 2016[12]).

Third, the Kyrgyz Republic has a large informal sector with two-thirds of the total workforce estimated to work informally, 80% of them in agriculture (OECD/ILO, 2017[13]). For the financial services sector, this means that most transactions are cash-based without need for a bank account. It also means people may feel they lack the needed documents to open a bank account (e.g. wage slips) (Hasanova, 2018[14]; OECD, 2019[6]). Opening a bank account, however, is free of charge and only requires a passport at many Kyrgyz banks. Therefore, a lack of a wage slip should not be an obstacle.

There are also informal financial service providers such as pawnshops, moneylenders or relatives where people borrow money (Hasanova, 2018[14]). The informality is strongly driven by the lack of trust in banks mentioned previously. Some Kyrgyz villages still practise a rotating savings and credit system established in Soviet times that involves close relatives, friends or neighbours. In this system, known as "chyornaya kassa", members pay into a common pot over a predefined period of time (Mamadiyarov, 2018[15];

Ibraimova, 2009[16]). At the group's regular meetings, the pot's lump sum is given in turn to each contributor for their personal use until every member has had a turn in using the funds (Mamadiyarov, 2018[15]). The system relies exclusively on trust among its members, which can be a powerful tool to sanction misbehaviour such as default. It has been set up specifically to avoid reliance on formal banking institutions (Mamadiyarov, 2019[17]; Imami, Rama and Polese, 2020[18]).

It is unlikely these informal credit systems compete directly with those offered through formal financial institutions. This is especially true in light of the distrust towards banks and lack of access to formal financial institutions in rural areas (see point four). Rather, these informal systems suggest the need to improve the supply of formal financial products and services that are seen as viable and attractive alternatives. At the same time, these practices show that people in Kyrgyzstan do have experience with financial products and services, if not formal ones. Commercial banks and other financial operators can build on existing experience to improve financial literacy.

Fourth, access to banking facilities is a big barrier. Penetration of bank branches and services, although expanding, remains restricted (OECD, 2019[6]). Five commercial bank branches are available per 100 000 Kyrgyz adults on average (Table 2.1). Branch distribution varies depending on oblast but overall lags behind other countries in the region. In Europe and Central Asia (excluding high-income countries), 25 branches are available per 100 000 adults on average (IMF, 2020[19]). People in remote areas in Kyrgyzstan in particular have limited access to banking services, including payment and transfer services and deposit facilities. High costs associated with operating branches in rural areas pose a major obstacle to increasing access to physical banking infrastructure (OECD, 2019[6]).

Table 2.1. Availability of bank branches per oblast

Oblast	Population 2019 in thousands	Bank branches	Bank branches per 100 000 inhabitants
Issyk-Kul	496.1	39	8
Bishkek	1053.9	74	7
Talas	267.4	18	7
Naryn	289.6	18	6
Batken	537.3	23	4
Chui	959.8	36	4
Jalal-Abad	1 238.8	46	4
Osh+Osh city	1 680.6	61	4
Total	6 523.5	315	5

Source: Own calculations; adapted from The National Bank of the Kyrgyz Republic (2020), National Bulletin 09/2020 (data), https://www.nbkr.kg; National Statistical Committee of the Kyrgyz Republic (2020), Permanent population of the Kyrgyz Republic in 2020 (data), http://www.stat.kg/en/statistics/naselenie/.

In sum, the evidence to date shows that parts of the Kyrgyz population save money or have experience with borrowing money but have limited use of formal financial services. Lack of physical banking infrastructure adds additional barriers. The OECD household survey collects more evidence on the barriers. The next two sections lay out the rationale for overcoming obstacles to wider access to and use of financial products and services, as well as proposing measures to do so. Subsequently, the survey design is presented.

Increasing access to and use of financial products and services

Wider and deeper penetration of banking services can help with economic development. Households or firms find it difficult to finance significant investments without access to financial markets because their own capital is usually limited. While not a substitute for functioning social policy and support, the ability to access financial services, including external finance, therefore can help expand opportunities for those with less financial and social capital (e.g. a social network/ connections), for poverty alleviation and for allowing new firms to access the market (World Bank, 2014[20]; Yoshino and Morgan, 2017[21]). In particular, poorer households can benefit from instruments to manage cash more efficiently and to smooth consumption (Yoshino and Morgan, 2017[21]; World Bank, 2014[20]). While credit can help households to address risks, it cannot act as a substitute for a functioning welfare state that protects vulnerable groups from social, economic and health risks (Wiedemann, 2021[22]).

Ensuring that households and firms have access to and use financial services is a precondition of an efficient economy. In addition, increased transparency associated with electronic funds transfers can help reduce corruption (Yoshino and Morgan, 2017[21]), and thus help increase trust in the (financial) system. Evidence has shown that lacking access to financial market services restrains the growth of small entrepreneurs who lack collateral, credit histories and connections (Aterido, Hallward-Driemeier and Pagés, 2011[23]; Beck, Demirguc-Kunt and Martinez Peria, 2005[24]). Empirical evidence has also confirmed this relationship holds true in the other direction, i.e. small firms grow faster in more financially developed markets (Beck et al., 2008[25]). Improving their access to finance is associated with innovation, job creation and growth (World Bank, 2014[20]). This is relevant for Kyrgyzstan with its high share of individual entrepreneurs and SMEs, as discussed above.

Financial depth, i.e. the availability of financial instruments to investors and the existence of sound financial institutions, contributes to growth (Mahmood and Rehman, 2019[26]; Masoud and Hardaker, 2012[27]). Existing evidence stresses, however, that regulatory and supervisory authorities need enough expertise to manage the expansion of the financial sector for growth to materialise (Rioja and Valev, 2004[28]). Relevant for the Kyrgyz context, higher penetration of bank branches and automated teller machines (ATMs) and wider use of loan services are generally associated with lower financing obstacles, even after controlling for financial sector depth (Beck, Demirguc-Kunt and Martinez Peria, 2005[24]).

Overcoming challenges in the banking sector

There are multiple ways to increase access to and use of financial products and services. Some instruments increase financial literacy. Others provide affordable, targeted financial products by, for example, lowering credit risk, alleviating collateral constraints and pooling demand. Still other instruments increase trust in financial institutions and improve access to physical banking infrastructure. These four instruments are considered in turn in this section.

Increasing financial literacy

Financial literacy is the knowledge and ability to choose financial products and services that help people manage their capital adequately. Equipping users with more financial literacy can increase use of financial services. Kyrgyzstan has recognised the importance of improving financial literacy, adopting its Programme to Improve Financial Literacy in the Kyrgyz Republic for 2016-2020 in 2016. As of 2020, it was developing the National Financial Inclusion Strategy (2021-2024), which includes a component on financial literacy. As part of the existing Programme to Improve Financial Literacy, several education programmes target younger children and middle-aged adults to improve financial literacy. A website was developed (www.finsabat.kg) where people can inform themselves about different aspects of financial literacy, including budget planning and consumer protection rights. Training comics for children are accessible via the website. Employees of the National Bank travel to different regions and train teachers who give financial literacy classes at schools (Kudryavtseva, 2019[29]). As of 2019, about 500 teachers had been trained and teach financial literacy classes to students (Kudryavtseva, 2019[29]). In addition, financial education centres are being trialled in 17 rural areas in pilots run by the National Bank and the United Nations Development Programme (Kudryavtseva, 2019[29]).

When the national Programme to Improve Financial Literacy is developed for the years after 2020, it can build on and scale up these important steps. Overall, the training materials need to explain clearly why and how financial institutions are safer and cheaper to use compared to cash-based transactions or informal services. In doing so, financial literacy should be connected to other socio-economic development goals. For example, financial literacy trainings and training materials could highlight the benefits of investing in clean technology or fuels, improved energy efficiency, more resilient crops or drip-irrigation for well-being and economic development.

Cases in other countries have shown that financial education per se is insufficient to get individuals to take up formal (or informal) financial products (World Bank, 2014[20]). However, combining general financial literacy interventions with measures that allow individuals to set their financial goals and get access to individualised financial counselling has benefits. This practice significantly increases take up of financial products such as bank accounts, reduces borrowing for private consumption and improves understanding of interest rates on loans (World Bank, 2014[20]; Carpena et al., 2017[30]).

There are other ways to scale up efforts to increase financial literacy in the Kyrgyz Republic. The country could develop mobile apps for financial management or promote existing ones. This would allow people to set their financial goals and track their spending on their mobile phones. It could set up individual financial counselling, including virtually for people in remote areas. Finally, it could engage commercial banks in these efforts.

Another country-wide example has shown that training community members as trainers of financial literacy achieves more change in saving behaviour than training loan officers as trainers (Hakizimfura, Randall and Zia, 2018[31]). The Kyrgyz programme mentioned above that trains teachers is a good example of engaging local community members. The National Bank could consider engaging other community members as well, such as shop owners.

Providing targeted and affordable financial products

Efforts to increase financial literacy must be backed up by attractive financial products that cater to the demands of potential clients, are affordable and are easy to understand. Supplementary financial instruments such as movable asset-based lending or credit guarantees could help alleviate collateral constraints. These options will be explored in more detail in Chapter 5.

Access to credit also improves when the legal, regulatory and institutional framework makes it easy to create and enforce collateral agreements and to increase information about potential borrowers' creditworthiness (World Bank, 2019[32]; OECD/ERIA, 2018[33]). Lenders look at a borrower's credit history and collateral. When reliable and relevant data on borrowers' credit histories are available, financial institutions are more likely to provide a loan (World Bank, 2019[32]). They can also charge lower interest rates because credit risk is lower. This is why credit reporting systems play an important role. They allow lenders to retrieve the credit histories of prospective borrowers and other registries that record the ownership and value of assets, both immovable and movable (OECD/ERIA, 2018[33]).

In Kyrgyzstan, the credit reporting agency was transformed from a public entity into a commercial one in 2003. The Ishenim Credit Bureau collects and stores data on the repayment history, unpaid debts or credit outstanding of listed individuals or firms to help reduce credit risks (Ishenim CJSC, 2020[34]). According to World Bank (2020[35]), the credit bureau holds information on credit histories of around 40% of adults in the Kyrgyz Republic. This is an encouraging number.

Expanding information collection to additional data providers could lead to more individuals and firms within the credit bureau's data. In Jamaica, for example, non-bank entities were included in the credit reporting regime (OECD/ERIA, 2018[36]). It significantly expanded the credit bureau's database to cover a wider section of consumers, including those without a bank account, and also increased the number of credit reports issued (OECD/ERIA, 2018[36]). In Kyrgyzstan, around 50 microfinance providers, 20 credit unions and 1 mobile service provider already contribute data to the Ishenim Credit Bureau (Ishenim CJSC, 2020[34]). Utility companies (e.g. water, electricity, telecommunications) and any other business that holds information on consumers' (re)payment histories could feed into the credit reporting regime and therefore increase coverage and depth of relevant information. Such businesses could include mobile service providers, as well as the remaining microfinance institutions that operate in the Kyrgyz Republic.

Kyrgyzstan also has a land registry in place, as part of the State Agency for Land Resources under the Kyrgyz government. Local offices hold data on immovable assets, i.e. land and real estate. According to World Bank Group (2020[37]), it is easy to register property in Kyrgyzstan. Banks can request information on property rights by signing an agreement with the State Agency and against a fee. They can access the data on line. Overall, it seems like Kyrgyzstan has working credit reporting systems that provide a strong base for increasing depth and coverage of information. In general, credit reporting should be underpinned by a strong legal framework that provides for credit information sharing among lenders and restricts access to customers' information without their consent (OECD/ERIA, 2018[36]).

Credit risk for lenders can be reduced in several ways. Access to reliable and comprehensive asset registries is one option. In addition, comprehensive and strong creditor rights and secured transaction frameworks will guarantee partial repayment in the event of loan default (OECD/ERIA, 2018[33]; World Bank, 2015[38]). Here, Kyrgyzstan still lacks an integrated or unified legal framework for secured transactions (World Bank Group, 2020[37]). There is also no specific, out-of-court compensation mechanism to cover for losses incurred by parties who engaged in good faith in a property transaction based on erroneous information certified by the immovable property registry (World Bank Group, 2020[37]).

Kyrgyzstan can try to improve the legal framework for creditors. Evidence from Indonesia has shown that financial institutions should be involved in the creation of a functioning transaction framework. This will ensure they see it as a useful risk-management tool (World Bank Group, 2017[39]). Awareness-raising activities with government agencies and the public are also vital to promote financing based on movable assets (World Bank Group, 2017[39]).

Building trust

High quality service and affordable products and services also help increase trust in the banking system. Promoting the Kyrgyz deposit protection system more widely among potential clients of financial institutions would also increase trust.

Improving physical infrastructure

Improving the physical infrastructure for financial products and services would allow more people to access them. As one way to overcome barriers to setting up more local bank branches, existing physical infrastructure could be used to provide banking services. Local post offices, for example, could be adapted to offer at least limited financial services (European Investment Bank, 2012[40]) With 900 local outposts, post offices have much wider geographic coverage in the Kyrgyz Republic than commercial banks, microfinance institutions and credit unions combined (Fitzgeorge-Parker, 2018[11]).

Many among the Kyrgyz population frequently use stationary self-service payment terminals. The terminals are available in shopping centres, small shops, government agencies and financial institutions across Kyrgyz regions. In 2018, 20 licensed providers were operating over 4 000 terminals (Hasanova, 2018[14]). They allow users to pay for their mobile and Internet providers, utilities and cable TV; to top up their electronic accounts, including some financial accounts (e.g. bank accounts from commercial bank Bai Tushum); and to pay back credit (FINCAbank, 2015[41]). The volume of operations with self-service terminals constituted 52% of the non-cash money stock in 2016, exceeding KGS 23 billion (Hasanova, 2018[14]). This indicates that terminals already provide an alternative to physical banking facilities such as ATMs and banking branches and also to digital services. Given these self-service terminals are widely accessible and popular, equipping them with basic deposit and transaction applications would be an easy way to increase access to financial services.

Increasing use of mobile banking (i.e. using a mobile device to access a financial account or make a financial transaction remotely) is another way to improve logistics of delivering banking services to households without building new bank branches. In remote areas of Kyrgyzstan, where ATMs and bank branches are frequently unavailable, mobile banking could increase penetration of banking services at a lower cost than physical infrastructure. This could be an option either while physical banking infrastructure is being set up or as a permanent alternative. This is particularly relevant for rural areas cut off for months at a time during winter. Currently, 4G networks cover over half of Kyrgyzstan (Paul Budde Communication, 2020[42]) whereas access to broadband Internet is still limited. Only 3% of the population had access to fixed broadband Internet in 2014 (and mainly in Bishkek) and 21% had access to wireless broadband (Digital Report, 2018[43]). While these numbers may be higher now, broadband connections will likely only be catching up with mobile networks.

References

Aterido, R., M. Hallward-Driemeier and C. Pagés (2011), "Big constraints to small firms' growth? Business environment and employment growth across firms", *Economic Development and Cultural Change*, Vol. 59/3, pp. 609-647, http://dx.doi.org/10.1086/658349. [23]

Beck, T. et al. (2008), "Finance, firm size, and growth", *Journal of Money, Credit and Banking*, Vol. 40/7, pp. 1379-1405, http://dx.doi.org/10.1111/j.1538-4616.2008.00164.x. [25]

Beck, T., A. Demirguc-Kunt and M. Martinez Peria (2005), "Reaching out : Access to and use of banking services across countries", *Journal of Financial Economics*, Vol. 85/1, pp. 234-266, https://doi.org/10.1016/j.jfineco.2006.07.002. [24]

Carpena, F. et al. (2017), "The ABCs of financial education: Experimental evidence on attitudes, behavior, and cognitive biases", *Management Science*, Vol. 65/1, pp. 346-369, https://doi.org/10.1287/mnsc.2017.2819 (accessed on 6 June 2020). [30]

Demirgüç-Kunt, A. et al. (2018), *The Global Findex Database 2017: Measuring Financial Inclusion and the Fintech Revolution*, (database), https://databank.worldbank.org/source/global-financial-inclusion (accessed on 12 February 2020). [10]

Digital Report (2018), "Kyrgyzstan: State of Affairs report", *Country Snapshot*, https://digital.report/kyrgyzstan-state-of-affairs-report/#_ftn14 (accessed on 17 September 2020). [43]

European Investment Bank (2012), *Banking in the Eastern Neighbours and Central Asia*, https://www.eib.org/attachments/efs/economic_report_banking_enca_en.pdf. [40]

FINCAbank (2015), "Payment Terminals", webpage, https://www.fincabank.kg/en/financial-literacy-articles/payment-terminals/ (accessed on 14 February 2020). [41]

Fitzgeorge-Parker, L. (2018), "Impact Banking: Microfinance Comes of Age in Kyrgyzstan", webpage, https://www.euromoney.com/article/b1b0967crmxs3m/impact-banking-microfinance-comes-of-age-in-kyrgyzstan?copyrightInfo=true (accessed on 8 March 2020). [11]

Hakizimfura, E., D. Randall and B. Zia (2018), "Decentralized delivery of financial education: Evidence from a country-wide field experiment", *Policy Research Working Paper*, No. 8521, World Bank, Washington, DC, http://hdl.handle.net/10986/29994. [31]

Hasanova, S. (2018), "Financial inclusion, financial regulation, financial literacy, and financial education in the Kyrgyz Republic", *Working Paper*, No. 850, Asian Development Bank Institute, Tokyo, https://www.adb.org/publications/financial-inclusion-regulation-literacy-education-kyrgyz-republic. [14]

Holzhacker, H. and D. Skakova (2019), *Kyrgyz Republic Diagnostic*, European Bank for Reconstruction and Development, London, https://www.ebrd.com/documents/policy/country-diagnostic-paper-kyrgyz-republic.pdf?blobnocache=true. [4]

Ibraimova, A. (2009), *Legal and Institutional Framework for Empowerment of Rural Communities in the Kyrgyz Republic*, Institute of Federalism, Fribourg, Switzerland, https://books.google.fr/books/about/Legal_and_Institutional_Framework_for_Em.html?id=ZSn KVoOERakC&redir_esc=y. [16]

Imami, D., K. Rama and A. Polese (2020), "Informality and access to finance during socialism and transition – the case of the rotating savings and credit schemes", *Journal of Evolutionary Economics*, Vol. 30, pp. 1367-1383, https://doi.org/10.1007/s00191-020-00679-3. [18]

IMF (2020), *Commercial Bank Branches (per 100,000 adults)*, (database), https://data.worldbank.org/indicator/FB.CBK.BRCH.P5?contextual=region&end=2019&name_desc=true&start=2004&view=chart (accessed on 30 November 2020). [19]

Ishenim CJSC (2020), "History", webpage, http://www.ishenim.kg/en/Page/History (accessed on 27 June 2020). [34]

Kudryavtseva, T. (2019), "Public confidence in financial system growing in Kyrgyzstan", 8 April, 24KG, https://24.kg/english/114216_Public_confidence_in_financial_system_growing_in_Kyrgyzstan /. [29]

Mahmood, M. and K. Rehman (2019), "Did capital market development and financial depth contribute to growth? Evidence from European financial integration", *European Review*, Vol. 27/4, pp. 506-518, http://dx.doi.org/doi:10.1017/S1062798719000164. [26]

Mamadiyarov, I. (2019), *Trust and Informal Financial Institutions in Central Asia: The Case of Kyrgyzstan*, Institut national des langues et civilisations orientales and French Institute for Central Asian Studies, Paris, https://lifeinkyrgyzstan.org/wp-content/uploads/sites/9/2019/10/13.4.Mamadiiarov_Eng.pdf. [17]

Mamadiyarov, I. (2018), "Better from a friend or from a bank? Kyrgyzstan between informal and formal financial services", 17 June, openDemocracy, https://www.opendemocracy.net/en/odr/kyrgyzstan-between-informal-and-formal-financial-services/. [15]

Masoud, N. and G. Hardaker (2012), "The impact of financial development on economic growth", *Studies in Economics and Finance*, Vol. 29/3, pp. 148-173, http://dx.doi.org/10.1108/10867371211246830. [27]

National Bank of the Kyrgyz Republic (2020), *Bulletin of the National Bank of the Kyrgyz Republic*, No. 9, National Bank of the Kyrgyz Republic, Bishkek, https://www.nbkr.kg/index1.jsp?item=137&lang=ENG. [8]

National Bank of the Kyrgyz Republic (2020), "List of Commercial Banks of the Kyrgyz Republic and Number of their Branches", webpage, https://www.nbkr.kg/index1.jsp?item=69&lang=ENG (accessed on 30 November 2020). [5]

National Bank of the Kyrgyz Republic (2018), *Main Directions for Development of the Microfinance Sector in the Kyrgyz Republic for 2018-2021*, National Bank of the Kyrgyz Republic, Bishkek, https://www.nbkr.kg/contout.jsp?item=3206&lang=ENG&material=84608. [9]

National Statistical Committee of the Kyrgyz Republic (2020), "Main indicators of activity of small and medium enterprises in January-September 2019-2020", in *Official Statistics (Small and medium enterprises)*, National Statistical Committee of the Kyrgyz Republic, Bishkek, http://www.stat.kg/en/statistics/maloe-i-srednee-predprinimatelstvo/. [3]

OECD (2019), *Roadmap for a National Strategy for Financial Education in Kyrgyz Republic*, https://www.oecd.org/education/financial-education-cis.htm. [6]

OECD (2018), "Business environment in Central Asia: Access to finance", in *Enhancing Competitiveness in Central Asia*, OECD Publishing, Paris, https://dx.doi.org/10.1787/9789264288133-5-en. [7]

OECD/ERIA (2018), *SME Policy Index: ASEAN 2018: Boosting Competitiveness and Inclusive Growth*, SME Policy Index, OECD Publishing, Paris/Economic Research Institute for ASEAN and East Asia, Jakarta, https://dx.doi.org/10.1787/9789264305328-en. [33]

OECD/ERIA (2018), *SME Policy Index: ASEAN 2018: Boosting Competitiveness and Inclusive Growth*, SME Policy Index, OECD Publishing, Paris/Economic Research Institute for ASEAN and East Asia, Jakarta, https://dx.doi.org/10.1787/9789264305328-en. [36]

OECD/ILO (2017), *How Immigrants Contribute to Kyrgyzstan's Economy*, International Labour Organization, Geneva/OECD Publishing, Paris, https://dx.doi.org/10.1787/9789264287303-en. [13]

Paul Budde Communication (2020), "Kyrgyzstan gains momentum in 4G rollouts", *Kyrgyzstan - Telecoms, Mobile and Broadband - Statistics and Analyses*, https://www.marketreportsonline.com/56352.html (accessed on 17 September 2020). [42]

Rioja, F. and N. Valev (2004), "Does one size fit all? A re-examination of the finance and growth relationship", *Journal of Development Economics*, Vol. 74/2, pp. 429–447, https://doi.org/10.1016/j.jdeveco.2003.06.006. [28]

The World Bank (2020), "Private credit bureau coverage (% of adults) - Kyrgyz Republic", *World Bank Open Data*, (database), https://data.worldbank.org/indicator/IC.CRD.PRVT.ZS?locations=KG (accessed on 27 June 2020). [35]

Tovar-García, E. and R. Kozubekova (2016), "The third pillar of the Basel Accord: Evidence of borrower discipline in the Kyrgyz banking system", *Journal of Eurasian Studies*, Vol. 7/2, pp. 195-204, https://doi.org/10.1016/J.EURAS.2016.02.002. [12]

Wiedemann, A. (2021), "A Social Policy Theory of Everyday Borrowing: On the Role of Welfare States and Credit Regimes", *American Journal of Political Science*, https://doi.org/10.1111/ajps.12632.   [22]

World Bank (2020), *Enterprise Surveys*, (database), http://www.enterprisesurveys.org (accessed on 2 August 2020).   [2]

World Bank (2019), *Global Financial Development Database: October 2019 Version*, World Bank, Washington, DC, https://www.worldbank.org/en/publication/gfdr/data/global-financial-development-database (accessed on 11 February 2020).   [32]

World Bank (2015), *Principles for Effective Insolvency and Creditor/Debtor Regimes, Revised 2015*, World Bank, Washington, DC, https://doi.org/10.1596/23356.   [38]

World Bank (2014), *Global Financial Development Report: Financial Inclusion*, World Bank, Washington, DC, http://dx.doi.org/10.1596/978-0-8213-9985-9.   [20]

World Bank Group (2020), *Doing Business 2020: Kyrgyz Republic*, World Bank, Washington, DC, https://www.doingbusiness.org/content/dam/doingBusiness/country/k/kyrgyz-republic/KGZ.pdf.   [37]

World Bank Group (2017), *Expanding Access to Finance for Small-Scale Businesses: Secured Transactions Reform: An Indonesia Case Study*, World Bank, Washington, DC, https://openknowledge.worldbank.org/handle/10986/25826.   [39]

Yamano, T. et al. (2019), *Kyrgyz Republic: Improving Growth Potential*, Asian Development Bank, Mandaluyong City, The Philippines, https://www.adb.org/publications/kyrgyz-republic-improving-growth-potential.   [1]

Yoshino, N. and P. Morgan (2017), "Overview of financial inclusion, regulation, and education", in Yoshino, N. and P. Morgan (eds.), *Financial Inclusion, Regulation, and Education: Asian Perspectives*, Asian Development Bank Institute, Tokyo, https://www.adb.org/sites/default/files/publication/350186/adbi-financial-inclusion-regulation-education-asian-perspectives.pdf.   [21]

Note

[1] Financial development is defined as a combination of depth (size and liquidity of markets), access (ability of individuals and companies to access financial services) and efficiency (ability of institutions to provide financial services at low cost and with sustainable revenues, and the level of activity of capital markets) (Svirydzenka 2016 cited in Yamano et al., 2019).

3 Rationale and methodology for the survey

This chapter briefly describes the motivation for the household survey, noting the demand among the Kyrgyz population for financial products and services is poorly understood. It suggests better understanding can help commercial banks, as well as policy makers and central bankers, to design more targeted interventions. The chapter outlines methodology and content of the 2019 survey of 1 000 households on their access to and use of (green) financial products and services in the Kyrgyz Republic. It notes the survey helps fill a gap in evidence on access to and demand for green financial products and services in the Kyrgyz Republic, and supports developing solutions to promote green finance-related activities.

Rationale and methodology for the survey

The OECD household survey contributes significantly to knowledge about access to and use of financial services. It collected empirical evidence on how and whether people in Kyrgyzstan use and access formal financial services, including green finance. Evidence on the breadth of financial systems across countries has improved in recent years. Notably, the World Bank and Gallup Inc. conduct the *Findex* Survey in over 140 countries including Kyrgyzstan. In Kyrgyzstan, the National Bank also collects evidence on indicators such as penetration of bank branches and automated teller machines. The 2019 *Life in Kyrgyzstan* survey, a nationally representative longitudinal survey of households, contributes information on household behaviour, including spending and saving (Brück et al., 2014[1]).

The particular demands of the Kyrgyz population for financial products and services, however, are still little understood. Although green finance is an emerging trend, knowledge on the appetite for green financial products and services in Kyrgyzstan is almost inexistent. The OECD prepared this household survey to close this gap in evidence. A better understanding can help commercial banks, as well as policy makers and central bankers, to design more targeted interventions. These can ultimately increase access to and use of financial products and services, including green finance, for the people of the Kyrgyz Republic.

Following a request from the National Bank of the Kyrgyz Republic, the OECD prepared a household survey to identify i) needs and demand for financial instruments among existing and potential clients of Kyrgyz financial institutions; and ii) solutions to promote finance-related activities contributing to sustainable development.

The survey, which took place in August 2019, included face-to-face interviews with 1 000 households across Kyrgyzstan on their use of banking services. As the first stage of selecting respondents (sample), the survey identified primary sampling units, i.e. households. These units were stratified by population size in each region. Sample selection was based on probabilities proportional to population size in each region. All household members eligible for the survey (aged 18-64) were sorted by gender and then by age. The Kish grid method was used to randomly select the respondent in each household. The method avoids selection bias by assigning an equal probability of selection for each eligible member of the household. The survey did not consider respondents' socio-economic backgrounds in its sampling. However, the sample is representative of the distribution of the population across the Kyrgyz regions as well as urban and rural areas. Given that household access to banking facilities varies depending on whether people live in rural or urban settings, the survey makes an important attempt to represent the geographic distribution of the population.

The interviews were in Kyrgyz, Russian or Uzbek. Annex A provides detailed descriptions on the survey method and some implementation challenges. Annex B describes specificities of the sample, e.g. household characteristics, education and occupation, in more detail. Questionnaires in English and Kyrgyz can be found in Annex C and Annex D respectively.

References

Brück, T. et al. (2014), "Household survey data for research on well-being and behavior in Central Asia", *Journal of Comparative Economics*, Vol. 42/3, pp. 819-835, https://doi.org/10.1016/j.jce.2013.02.003. [1]

4 Key findings from the household survey

This chapter presents the results of the household survey. The survey covers experience with green financial instruments, access to and use of formal banking services, including credit and use of mobile banking. It also provides insights on differences in financial behaviour and experience by region, level of education and gender. The key findings shed light on the experience of households with formal financial instruments, including green instruments. It examines perceptions of respondents around barriers for taking out a green loan, including the role of high interest rates, short lending terms, insufficient collateral and inconvenient repayment schedules. It also explores other barriers such as awareness, knowledge and understanding of green investment.

Experience with and attitude towards green financial products

The survey shows that 30% of households have taken out money to finance activities with a climate mitigation or adaptation purpose in the past five years (Figure 4.1). Few (1%) respondents said they had invested in switching to crops that are more resilient to changing climate or weather or with less environmental impact (e.g. protect the soil, biodiversity, ecosystem services etc.). The same number (1%) said they financed improvement of their water use (e.g. more efficient irrigation systems, better access to clean water, etc.). More respondents (2%) said they had taken out a loan to finance energy-saving measures (e.g. house insulation, a more efficient boiler, etc.). Finally, 6% of respondents said they had invested in agriculture and disaster risk insurance. Switching livestock and crop varieties were the most common reasons and could make households more resilient and/or help increase production.

Figure 4.1. Households that have financed green investment activities

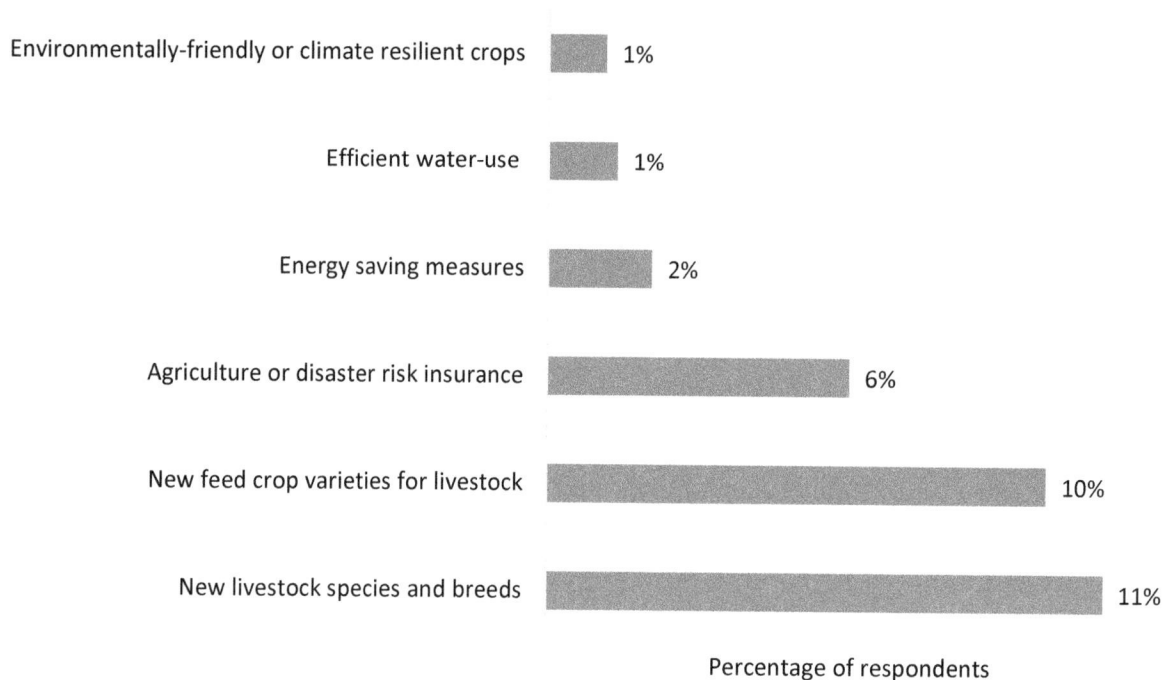

Percentage of respondents

Note: Respondents were able to choose multiple answers (average number of answers per household: 1.114). Number of households: 438.
Source: OECD Kyrgyz Household Survey on Green Finance

Only 0.5% invested the loan to produce energy from renewable sources. The same number of respondents financed improvements in forest management (e.g. to reduce risk from wildfires). Only one household (0.2%) responded they had invested in wastewater management. No one reported taking out a loan to finance protection of biodiversity, improve waste management or reduce air pollution. Table 4.1 provides an overview of these and other purposes respondents had chosen for their loan.

Table 4.1. Reasons for taking out a loan

Other investment purposes	Response/households
Business development	8%
Build or buy a house	8%
No response	5%
Agricultural development, purchase of livestock	5%
Private consumption	5%
Purchase of electronic equipment or car	2%
Other activity	2%
Wedding or funeral	1%
Production of energy from renewable sources	0.5%
Forest management	0.5%
Wastewater management	0.2%
Waste management	0%
Protection of biodiversity	0%
Air pollution reduction	0%

Note: Respondents were able to choose multiple answers (average number of answers per household: 1.114). Number of households: 438.
Source: OECD Kyrgyz Household Survey on Green Finance

Types of green investment activities vary across oblasts (Figure 4.2).

In Talas, none of the respondents had invested in any green activities in the past five years. Similarly, in Osh city, the survey found little green investment behaviour. Bishkek is the only place where households said they had taken out a loan to invest in energy production from renewable sources (3.6% of total respondents in Bishkek, which corresponds to two households).

The two oblasts with the highest uptake of agriculture or disaster risk insurance are Osh and Jalal-Abad, followed by Chui. These oblasts have the most business entities (mostly individual entrepreneurs) engaged in agricultural production in Kyrgyzstan. In 2019, Osh oblast accounted for a significant proportion of such business entities – 125 000, or almost 28% of the total. Jalal-had more than 100 000 (or almost 23% of total agricultural entities) and Chui had almost 70 000 (or 15%) (National Statistical Committee of the Kyrgyz Republic, 2020[1]).

Agricultural producers are strongly impacted by weather-related events such as droughts, frost and hail, as well as disasters such as floods and landslides. Consequently, they have incentives to insure against agricultural losses. Many respondents also said they had invested in new livestock species and breeds and new feed crop varieties. Batken is the region with the largest proportion of respondents taking out a loan to finance new livestock species and breeds (37.5%), followed by Jalal-Abad and Chui. Overall, little to no diversity in green investment activity can be detected in Talas, Osh city and Batken apart from investment in new livestock species and breeds and new feed crop varieties. The findings also show that respondents in the regions of Osh, Jalal-Abad and Chui were willing to take out loans for agricultural and disaster risk insurance. This suggests that insurance provision in these areas could be scaled up.

Figure 4.2. Distribution of households that have financed green investment activities per oblast

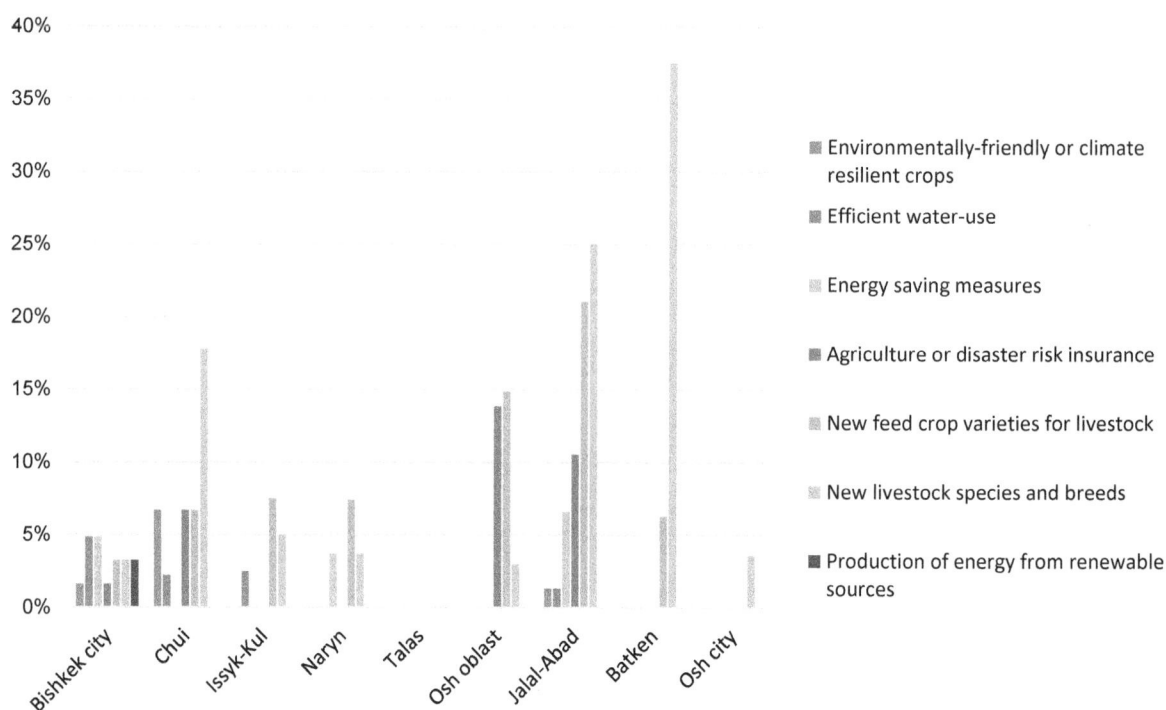

Source: OECD Kyrgyz Household Survey on Green Finance

Respondents were asked whether they would be interested in a loan or another financial instrument in the future to finance any activity related to climate adaptation or mitigation listed in Figure 4.1. Most (70%) said they did not know. The finding points to a clear gap in knowledge and understanding of the pros and cons of green investment and that respondents had not previously reflected on making green investments. In other findings, 14% of respondents would be interested in a loan to switch livestock, while 10% would use the loan for new and alternative feed crop varieties. In this regard, people who would be interested in a green loan have similar investment goals to those who already had a green loan.

There was some interest (more than 5%) to take out agricultural or other disaster risk insurance and to invest in energy efficiency measures (a little over 5%). Some respondents (3.6%) were interested in switching to more environmentally-friendly or resilient crop varieties and in investing in water management such as more efficient irrigation. Just under 3% of respondents would be interested in investing to reduce outdoor air pollution and to produce energy from renewable sources. These findings are important for commercial banks and the regulator. They point to demand for increased adaptation and mitigation measures these institutions could cater to and help grow. The regulator could consider whether to make such investment opportunities more attractive through direct or indirect support measures.

Few respondents were interested in investments in forest management or to protect biodiversity. This points to a need to raise awareness of the benefits of such activities.

Figure 4.3. Green investments households may wish to make in the future

Responses in percentages

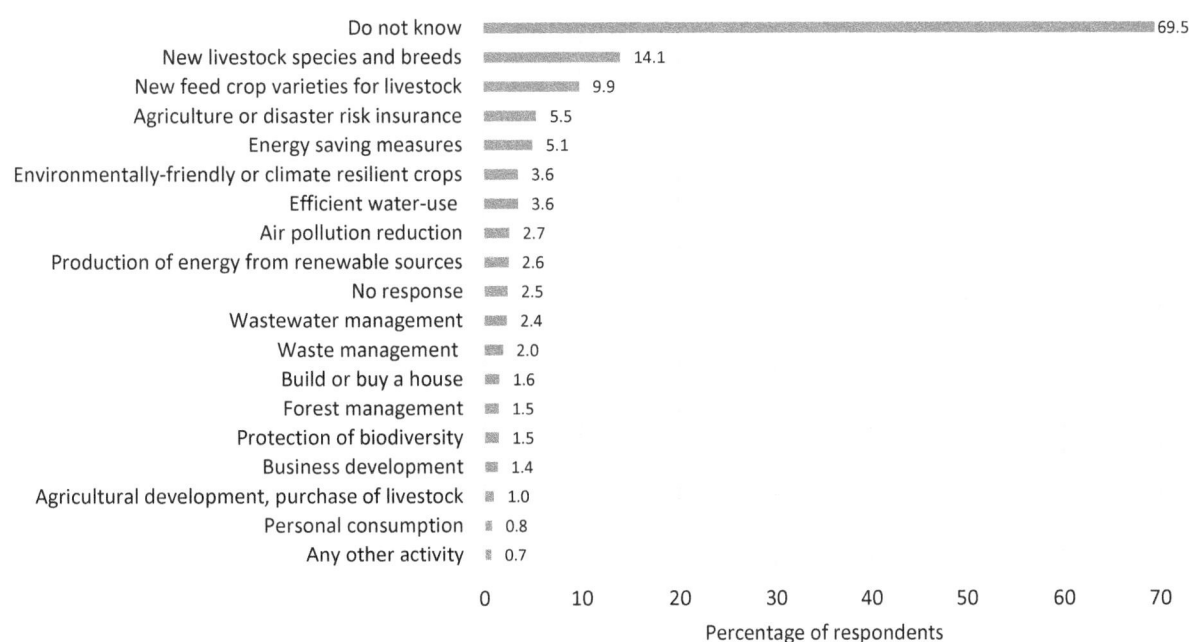

Category	Percentage
Do not know	69.5
New livestock species and breeds	14.1
New feed crop varieties for livestock	9.9
Agriculture or disaster risk insurance	5.5
Energy saving measures	5.1
Environmentally-friendly or climate resilient crops	3.6
Efficient water-use	3.6
Air pollution reduction	2.7
Production of energy from renewable sources	2.6
No response	2.5
Wastewater management	2.4
Waste management	2.0
Build or buy a house	1.6
Forest management	1.5
Protection of biodiversity	1.5
Business development	1.4
Agricultural development, purchase of livestock	1.0
Personal consumption	0.8
Any other activity	0.7

Percentage of respondents

Note: Respondents could choose multiple answers.
Source: OECD Kyrgyz Household Survey on Green Finance

Figure 4.4 shows a large majority of respondents are hypothetically interested in a green loan of up to USD 5 000 (KGS 35 000).

Figure 4.4. The amount of money households would like to borrow to finance green investments

Responses in percentages

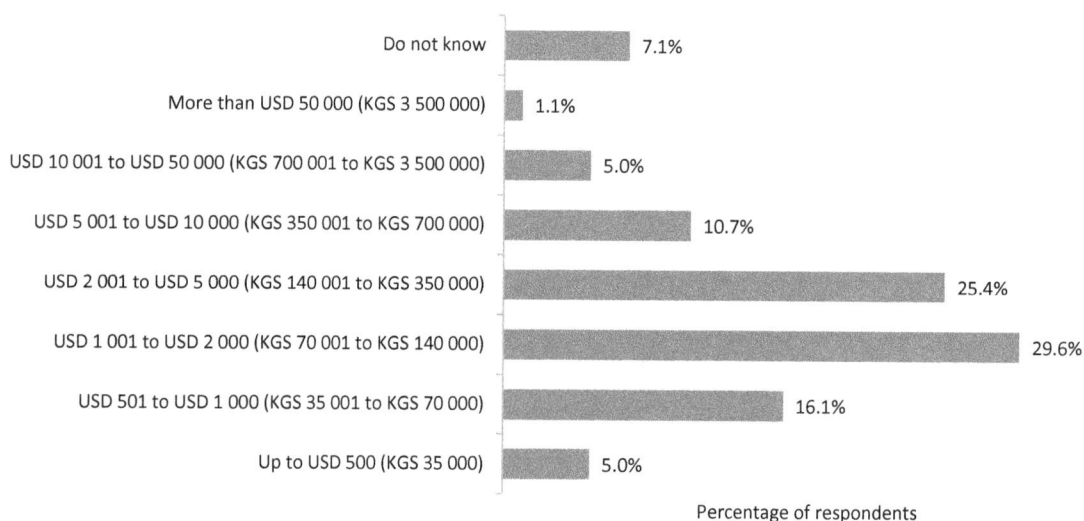

Source: OECD Kyrgyz Household Survey on Green Finance

The finding points to a clear gap in knowledge and understanding of the pros and cons of green investment and that respondents had not previously reflected on making green investments.

Respondents were asked to identify the theoretical barriers of taking out a green loan in the future (Figure 4.5). The answers show that respondents have a fairly informed understanding of the reality of borrowing money. The perceived barriers are similar to the ones listed by respondents who had taken out a loan Figure 4.21).

Respondents identified high interest rates as the biggest barrier to taking out a green loan. Around 30% thought they would face high interest rates if they took out a loan for green investments. In other findings, around 17% thought the lending term would be too short, while 10% responded that insufficient collateral poses a hypothetical barrier. Another 10% perceived the repayment schedule of green loans to be inconvenient. Almost 10% thought their insufficient knowledge on how to access and use banking services would hinder them from taking out a green loan.

Together with lack of bank accounts (around 6% of responses), lack of information on banking products (4.5%) and lack of information on purpose of green financial products (around 4%), these answers highlight the need to increase financial literacy, access to bank accounts and awareness of green financial products.

In all, 4% of people said they were afraid of integrity issues such as corruption. This percentage is significantly smaller than attitudes towards conventional loans (10% said they would not take out any financial product because they are afraid of corruption).

Figure 4.5. Perceived barriers that prevent households from taking out a green financial product in the future

Responses in percentages

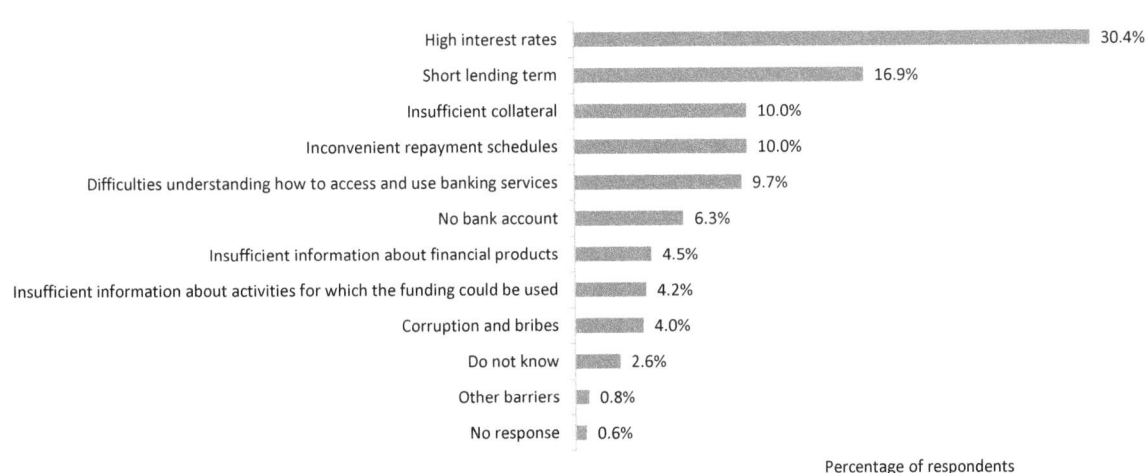

Note: Respondents were able to choose multiple answers.
Source: OECD Kyrgyz Household Survey on Green Finance

The survey sheds light on what drives lack of interest in green financial products (Figure 4.6). Almost 30% of respondents said they had no need for a financial product because they would use their own funding. Around 20% thought that green financial products would be too expensive or the equipment for them would be too expensive or unavailable in Kyrgyzstan (almost 8%). Almost 12% gave lack of sufficient information about green financial products and around 10% gave lack of information on funding purposes as reasons for their lack of interest. This answer points to the need for better information provision on green financial products. Around 4% said they had other funding priorities, while 2% said they were not interested in environmental protection or sustainable development. Only 3% gave lack of environmental regulation as a reason for not being interested. Religion played only a small role (0.3%) in preventing people from being interested in green financial products.

Figure 4.6. Reasons for not being interested in green financial products or services

Responses in percentages

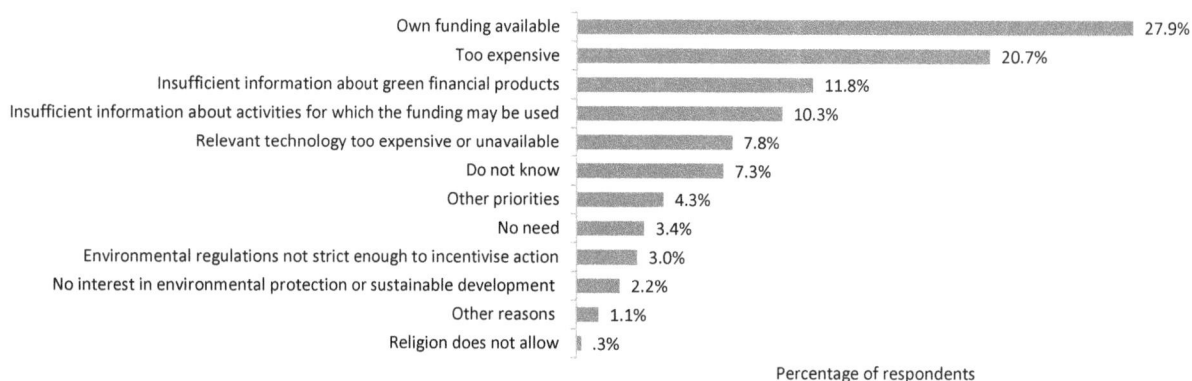

Own funding available	27.9%
Too expensive	20.7%
Insufficient information about green financial products	11.8%
Insufficient information about activities for which the funding may be used	10.3%
Relevant technology too expensive or unavailable	7.8%
Do not know	7.3%
Other priorities	4.3%
No need	3.4%
Environmental regulations not strict enough to incentivise action	3.0%
No interest in environmental protection or sustainable development	2.2%
Other reasons	1.1%
Religion does not allow	.3%

Percentage of respondents

Note: Respondents were able to choose multiple answers.
Source: OECD Kyrgyz Household Survey on Green Finance

Figure 4.7. Kinds of support people would like in order to use a green financial product

Responses in percentages

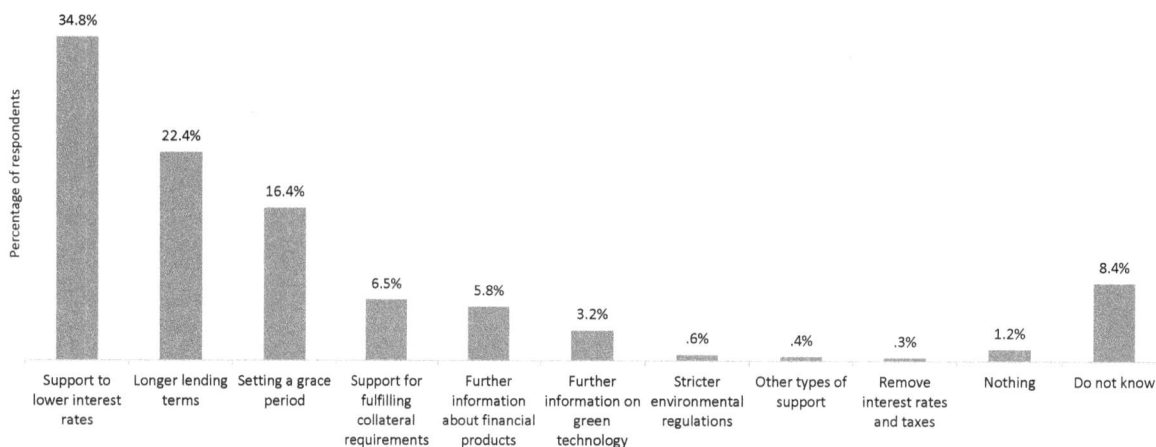

Support to lower interest rates	34.8%
Longer lending terms	22.4%
Setting a grace period	16.4%
Support for fulfilling collateral requirements	6.5%
Further information about financial products	5.8%
Further information on green technology	3.2%
Stricter environmental regulations	.6%
Other types of support	.4%
Remove interest rates and taxes	.3%
Nothing	1.2%
Do not know	8.4%

Note: Respondents chose multiple answers.
Source: OECD Kyrgyz Household Survey on Green Finance

Respondents were asked what types of support could incentivise them to finance green investments (Figure 4.7). The answers are in line with the perceived barriers identified and shown in Figure 4.5. Further, they point to greater roles for commercial banks (in combination with some rewriting of current lending terms). Specifically, banks could make their products more attractive and increase information flows of the types and purpose of different products.

Almost 35% wish for support to lower interest rates. This is in line with other findings that financing in the Kyrgyz Republic remains expensive (Yamano et al., 2019[2]). Furthermore, 22% wish for longer lending terms or a grace period to repay the loan (16%). These two findings point to the need for more patient capital and more lenient repayment schedules.

Given that collateral requirements are quite high in the Kyrgyz Republic, it is not surprising that 6.5% of respondents wanted support for collateral requirements. One would expect this number to be even higher, but collateral requirements are more significant for businesses who tend to ask for higher loans than households. In all, 9% of respondents wished for more information on green financial products.

Use of financial services

The OECD survey also investigated respondents' general financial behaviour and use of financial products and services. The results are presented in the following section. The number of depositors with commercial banks is low in the Kyrgyz Republic. The survey found that 81% of the 1 000 respondents did not have bank accounts (Figure 4.8). Slightly more women had bank accounts compared to men (21% of female respondents compared to 17% male; the reasons for this difference were not explored as part of the survey). The low number of bank accounts is likely driven by a mix of reasons such as lack of access, small amounts of savings, distrust in the financial system and alternative, informal means of using money. Chapter 2 has explored the underlying drivers further.

Figure 4.8. Respondents with and without a bank account, in percentage

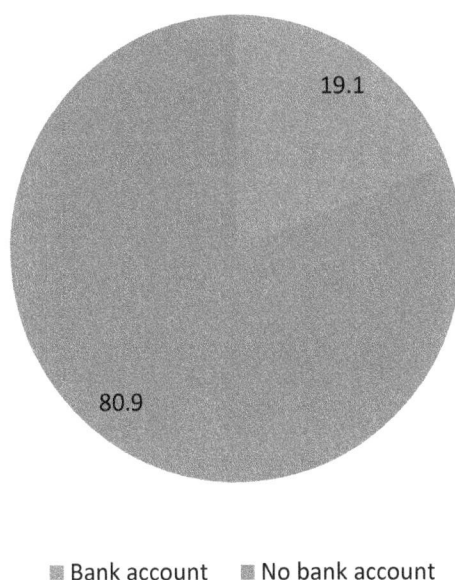

19.1

80.9

■ Bank account   ■ No bank account

Source: OECD Kyrgyz Household Survey on Green Finance

A household survey in Kyrgyzstan in 2017 by the World Bank also found high numbers of people without bank accounts (60%) (Demirgüç-Kunt et al., 2018[3]). Other data shows that the number of bank accounts per 1 000 adults in Kyrgyzstan increased from 15% in 2011 to slightly over 50% in 2017 (World Bank, 2019[4]). In the OECD survey, 65% of respondents live in rural areas, which represents the general distribution of the population between rural and urban settings in Kyrgyzstan. In rural areas, access to banks is restricted, as elaborated below (Figure 4.9). Therefore, lack of access could explain why this survey finds higher numbers of people without bank accounts compared to previous surveys.

Figure 4.9. Number and percentage of people with and without bank accounts by type of area

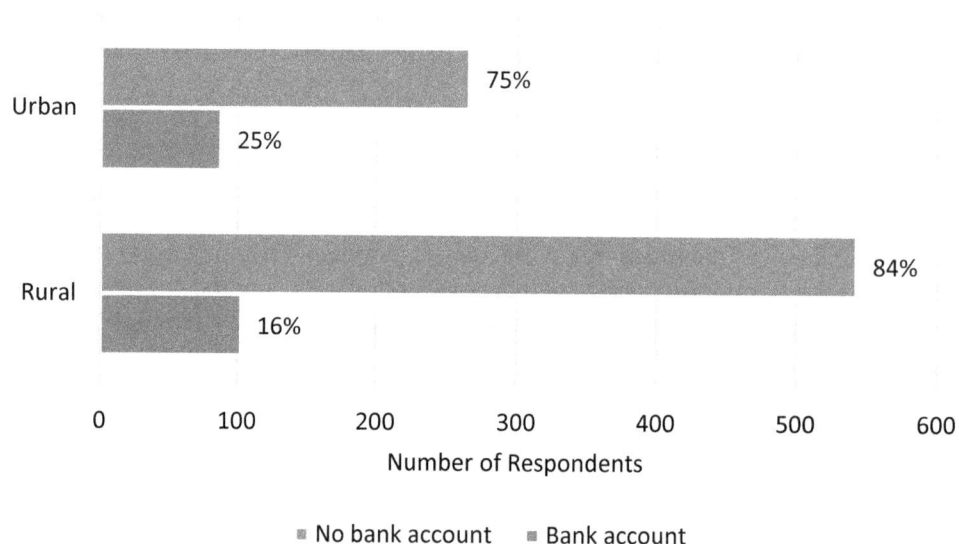

Source: OECD Kyrgyz Household Survey on Green Finance

The percentage of people without bank accounts across Kyrgyzstan is high, as stated above. The survey found that 25% of respondents in cities, however, do own a bank account compared to only 16% in rural areas. This empirically confirms statements from other studies that financial activity remains concentrated in larger cities (OECD, 2019[5]).

Figure 4.10. Percentage of people per oblast with a bank account

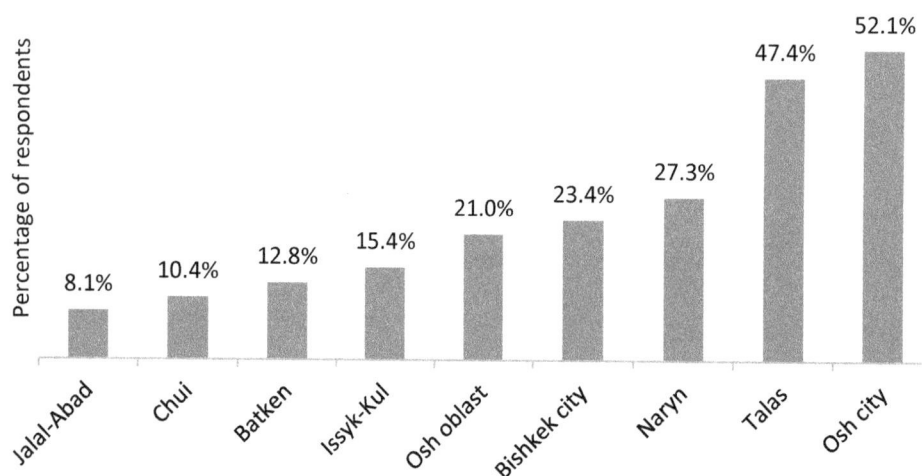

Source: OECD Kyrgyz Household Survey on Green Finance

Jalal-Abad, Chui and Batken are the regions with the lowest ownership of bank accounts (Figure 4.10). This can be partially explained by the low rate of bank services available in these regions (as shown in Table 2.1. in Chapter 2) and further explained in the next section). As mentioned above, more people with bank accounts live in larger towns and cities, i.e. Bishkek, Naryn, Talas and Osh where access is higher.

The education system of Kyrgyzstan consists of these levels: preprimary; secondary general (including primary); secondary technical and special; postsecondary non-higher; and higher education (OECD/ILO, 2017[6]; Ministry for Education, Science & Culture of the Kyrgyz Republic, 2000[7]).[1] The proportion of respondents without bank accounts is high across education levels, ranging between 60-96% (Figure 4.11). However, more people with college-level education (almost 40%) and higher education (over 30%) own bank accounts compared to those with lower education levels. Those with higher education levels may also have higher income levels and thus more incentives to deposit and invest money.

Figure 4.11. Percentage of respondents with and without bank accounts per education level

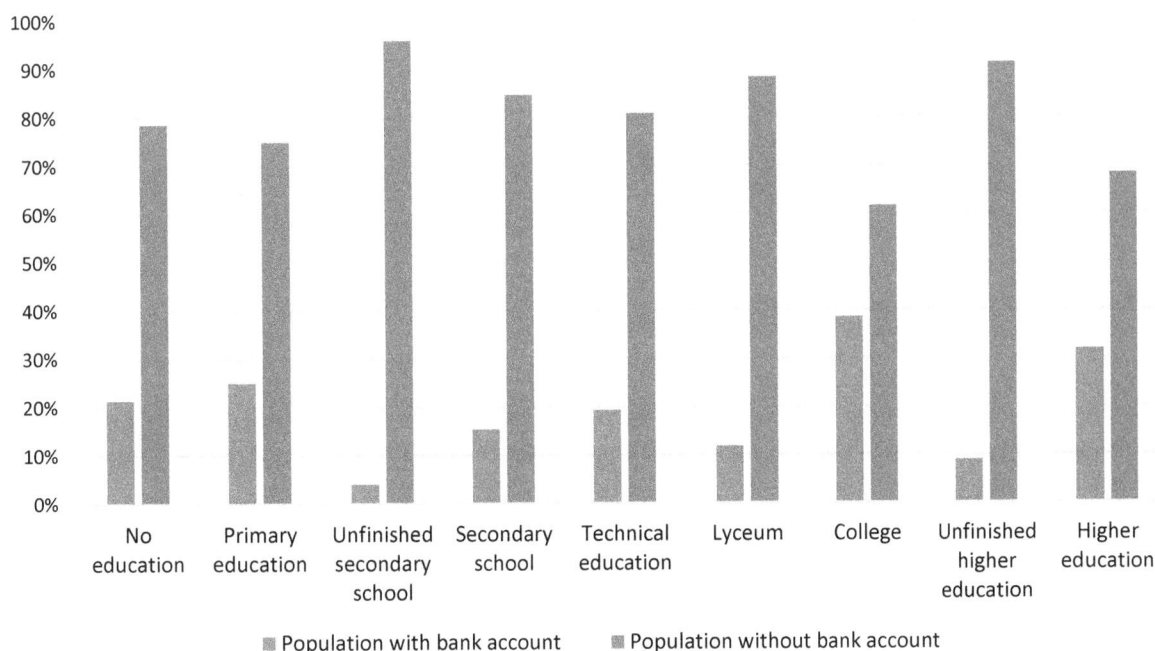

Source: OECD Kyrgyz Household Survey on Green Finance

Use of mobile banking

Mobile banking offers the advantage of accessing banking services anywhere at any time provided one has access to a mobile network and device. Mobile banking is defined here as using a mobile device to access a financial account or make a financial transaction remotely. Of those respondents with a bank account, 26% used mobile banking (Figure 4.12). This is a low percentage, but higher than that found in the *Global Findex* survey from 2017. According to the *Global Findex* results, only 10% with a financial institution account reported using a mobile phone or the Internet to access their account in the Kyrgyz Republic in the past 12 months in 2017 (Demirgüç-Kunt et al., 2018[3]).

Other research suggests that only slightly over 12% of the population use mobile phones for bank operations (Hasanova, 2018[8]). The OECD's study is more recent; few banks provided Internet-banking access through mobile applications back in 2017/18 (Hasanova, 2018[8]) whereas now most banks do. This can help explain the difference in findings. In any case, use of mobile banking and digital payments in general in Kyrgyzstan is found to be lower than in other countries in the region where 35% reported using mobile banking in 2017 (Demirgüç-Kunt et al., 2018[3]).

Figure 4.12. Use of mobile banking, in percentage

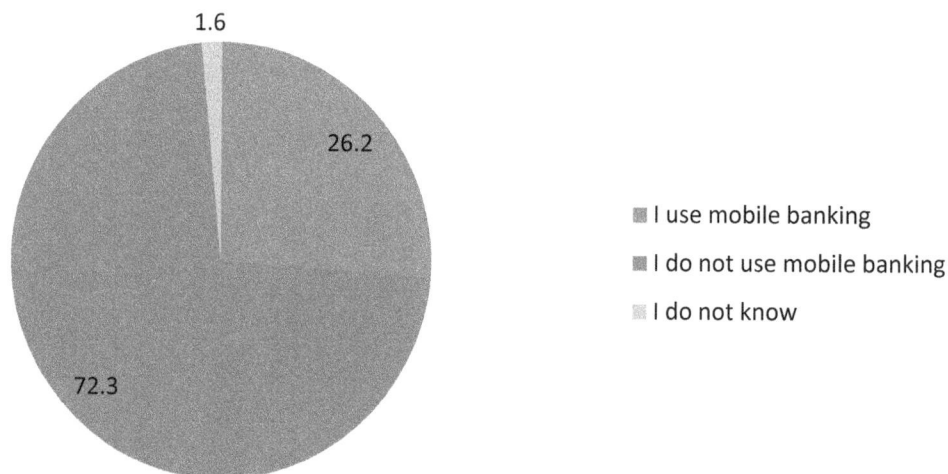

- I use mobile banking
- I do not use mobile banking
- I do not know

Note: The respondents here are those who have a bank account.
Source: OECD Kyrgyz Household Survey on Green Finance

There are regional differences (Figure 4.13). In Bishkek, more than 50% of respondents with a bank account use mobile banking. Use of mobile banking is even higher in Jalal-Abad (more than 70%) and Issy-Kul (more than 60%).

In Jalal-Abad, the comparatively lower access to physical banking infrastructure through bank branches (as shown in Table 2.1. in Chapter 2) might drive the higher percentage of people using mobile banking. In this case, mobile banking might substitute for lack of access to other banking infrastructure.

In Issy-Kul, however, access to physical banking infrastructure is less of a problem. Yet over 60% of respondents with a bank account still use mobile banking. Therefore, physical banking infrastructure might be less of a driver here.

In general, limited access to broadband Internet in rural areas restricts availability of digital services (Hasanova, 2018[8]). It could explain why mobile banking is not more widely used. However, it does not explain why uptake is low in metropolitan areas Naryn, Talas and Osh city. Lack of mobile banking applications and people using self-service terminals instead might be the bigger driver here.

Figure 4.13. Use of mobile banking per oblast, in percentage

Percentages of respondents who use mobile banking

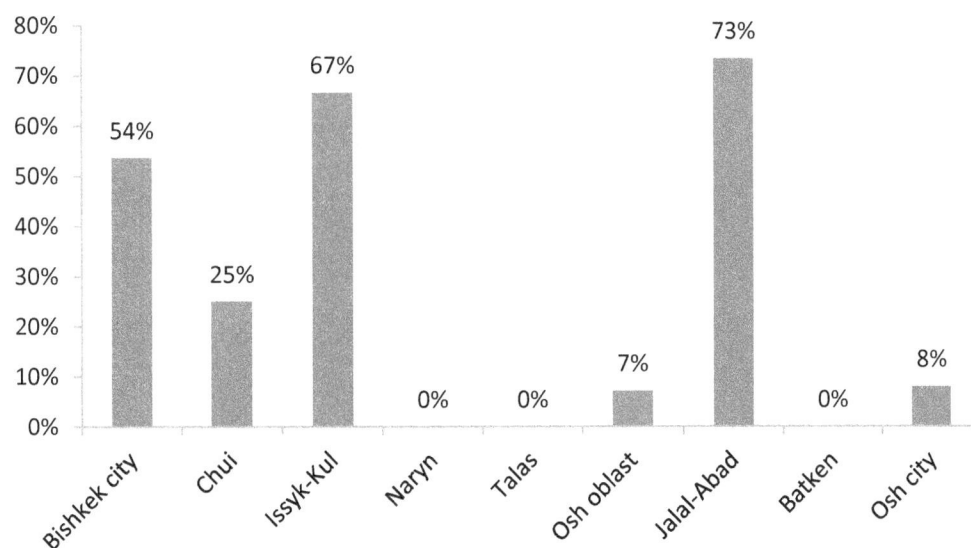

Note: The respondents here are those who have a bank account.
Source: OECD Kyrgyz Household Survey on Green Finance

As shown in Figure 4.14 and Figure 4.15, of those who use mobile banking, almost 70% of people with higher education levels (having at least achieved Lyceum level education or higher) use mobile banking.

Figure 4.14. Use of mobile banking by levels of education

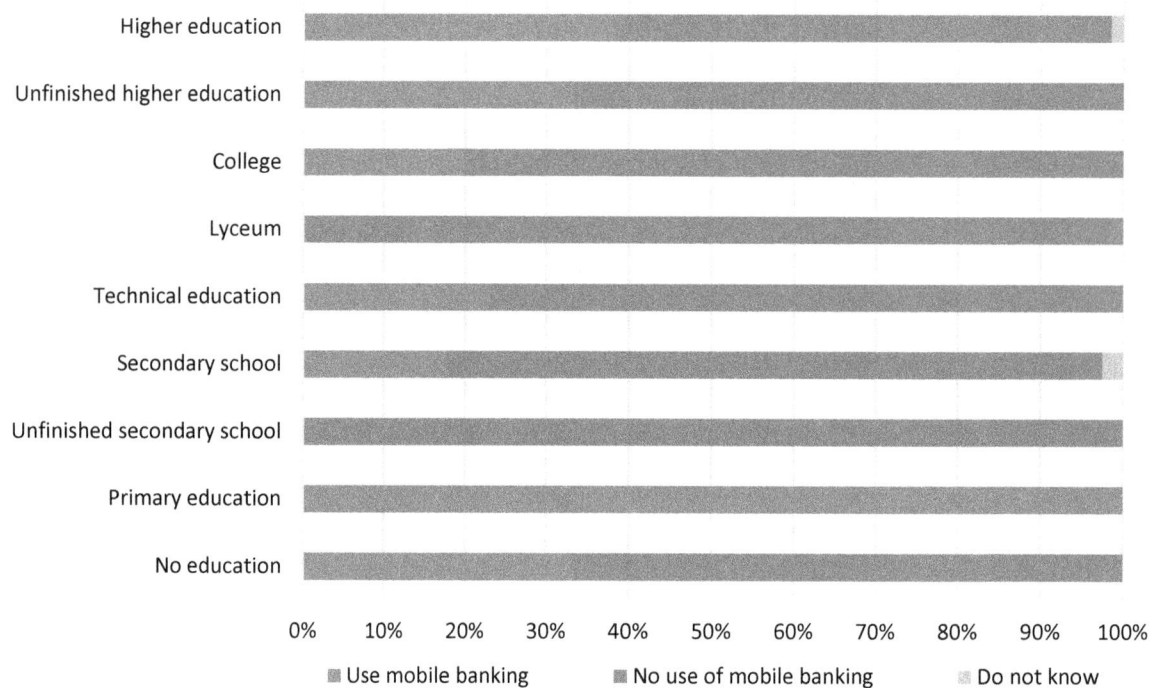

Note: The respondents here are those with a bank account.
Source: OECD Kyrgyz Household Survey on Green Finance

Figure 4.15. More people with higher education levels use mobile banking

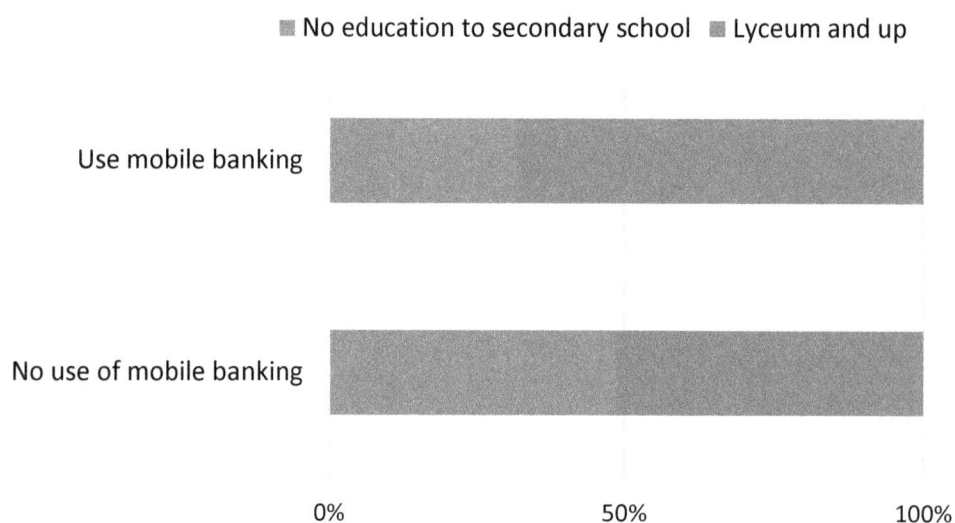

Note: The respondents here are those who have a bank account.
Source: OECD Kyrgyz Household Survey on Green Finance

Experience with loans

Credit forms an important part of economic development. It finances production, consumption and capital formation, which in turn affect economic activity (World Bank Group, 2020[9]). Credit to the private sector and households and their access to credit are therefore a development indicator. Only 14% of respondents said they took out a loan once and the same percentage did so repeatedly from a bank over the past five years (Figure 4.16). Around 11% took out a loan from a microfinance or microcredit institution once and 12% did so repeatedly over the past five years.

Respondents used microfinance/-credit institutions almost as often as banks. Credit unions, however, are used very little. Only around 1% of respondents took out a loan once or more than once from a credit union over the past five years. The findings show, nevertheless, that female loan takers used credit unions five times as often as male. Almost 2% of female respondents used credit unions compared to 0.4% male. The study did not explore the reasons for this difference.

Figure 4.16. Percentage of people who have taken out a loan in the past five years, by type of financial institution

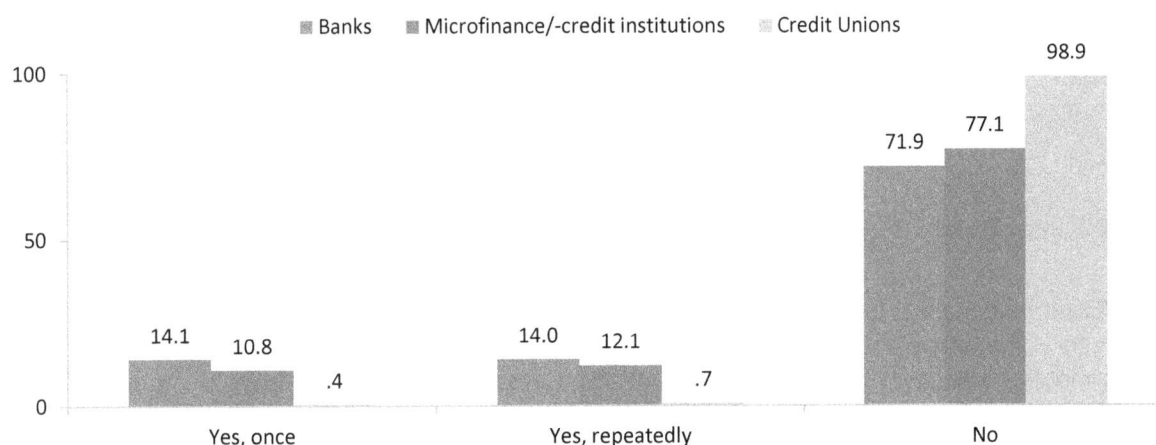

Note: Respondents in the first three columns have taken a loan once in the past five years; respondents in the middle three columns have taken a loan more than once in the past five years; respondents in the three right columns have not taken any loan in the past five years.
Source: OECD Kyrgyz Household Survey on Green Finance

Figure 4.17 shows the financial institutions used by respondents who took out a loan per oblast. It shows that use of banks did not strongly outweigh use of microfinance/- credit institutions or vice versa in any oblast.

Figure 4.17. Percentage of people who have taken out a loan once or repeatedly by location

Per type of financial service provider and per oblast

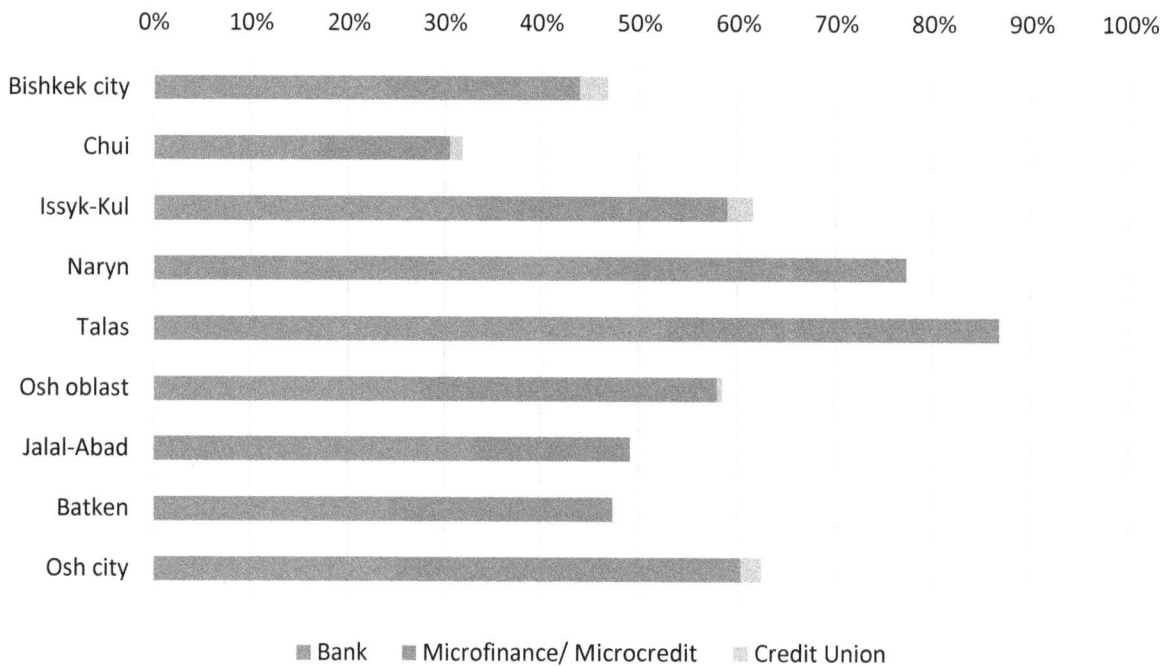

Source: OECD Kyrgyz Household Survey on Green Finance

In all, 92% of respondents took out a loan up to KGS 350 000 (USD 5 000) (Figure 4.18). Of those, 30% took a loan in the range of KGS 35 001-70 000 (USD 501-1 000), which is in the range of two to four average monthly salaries. Around 20% of respondents, respectively, took out loans up to KGS 35 000 (USD 500), loans ranging from KGS 70 001-140 000 (USD 1 001-2 000) and loans of between KGS 140 001-350 000 (USD 2 001-5 000). Around 8% took out loans of KGS 350 001 or higher.

Figure 4.18. Amount of loans taken

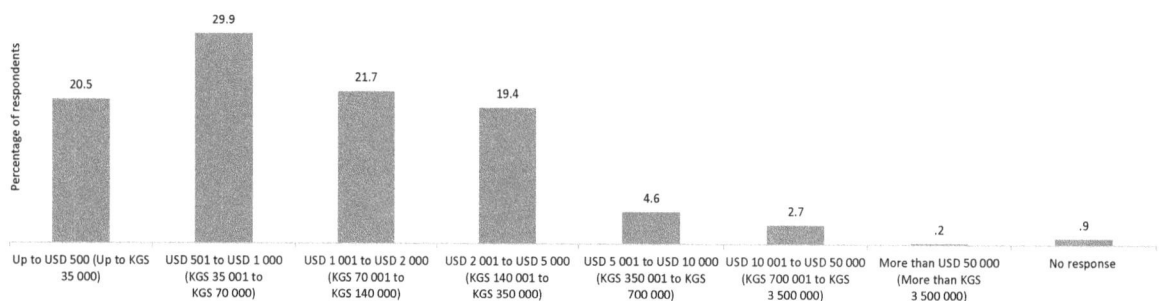

Note: The percentage of respondents are of those who took out a loan.
Source: OECD Kyrgyz Household Survey on Green Finance

The relatively small size of the loans already indicates that most respondents did not likely make major investments with the money. The overview below shows the main purpose for taking the loan (Figure 4.19). More than half of respondents wanted to cover private consumption, while almost 14% aimed to pay back a mortgage or undertake other housing expenditure, i.e. household investment. Almost 30% used the money for business reasons: around 19% took out a loan to cover operational business expenditure and just under 10% used the money to invest in their business. Around 4% of respondents took out a loan to pay back other debt.

Figure 4.19. Main purpose of the loan

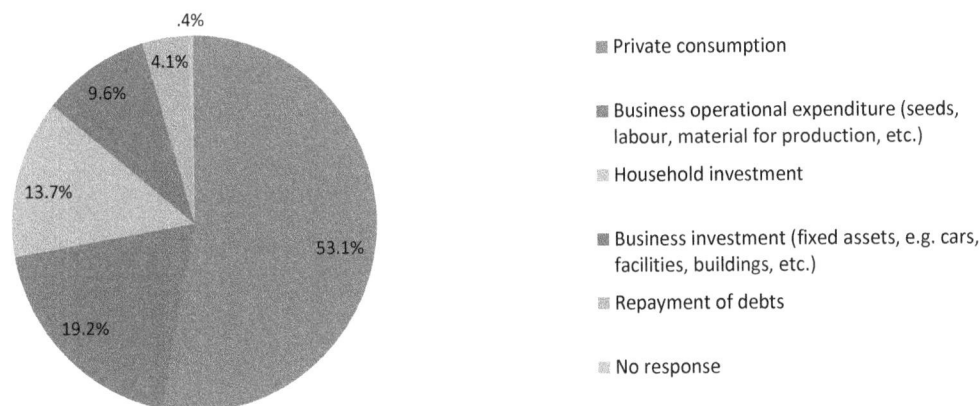

Source: OECD Kyrgyz Household Survey on Green Finance

Through a regional lens, the main reason for taking a loan is private consumption. As shown in Figure 4.20, more than 80% of respondents in Naryn took out a loan to finance private consumption. In Bishkek (22%) and in the Talas region (17%), more respondents borrowed to develop their business compared to other oblasts. Whereas in Jalal-Abad and Osh city, 12% and 14%, respectively, took out loans to develop their business, under 5% did so in Issy-Kul, Naryn and Batken. A significant share of respondents took out loans to support operational expenditure of their business in Chui (almost 30%), the Osh region (almost 30%), Jalal-Abad (26%) and Batken (almost 20%).

Figure 4.20. Reasons for taking out a loan, by region

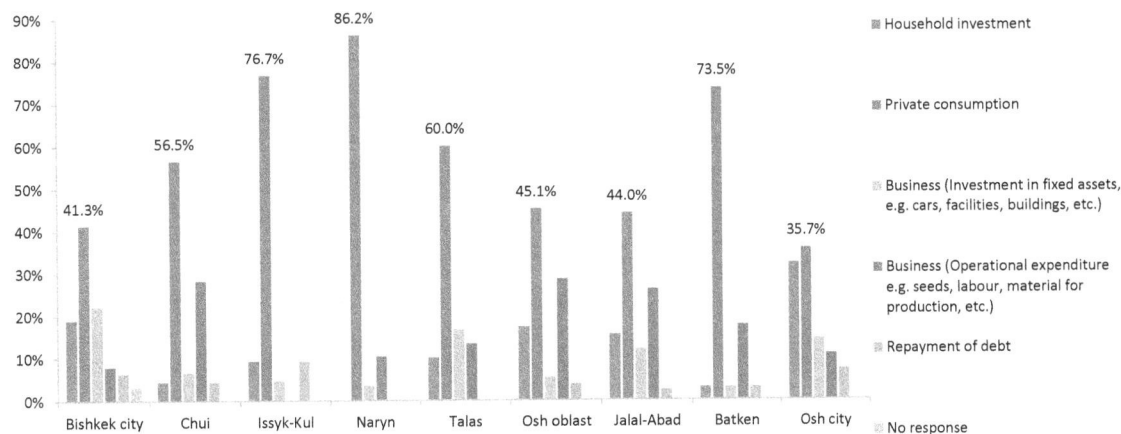

Source: OECD Kyrgyz Household Survey on Green Finance

As shown in Table 4.2, more than 20% of respondents in rural areas borrowed for operational expenditure compared to fewer than 10% of urban respondents. Urban respondents are almost three times more likely to borrow to invest in their business as rural respondents. One can interpret this in different ways. On the one hand, the definition of investment in fixed assets versus operational expenditure might be driving results. For rural agricultural producers, buying seeds or new livestock could be investing in an asset and increasing production. Thus, for agricultural producers, the definition of operational expenditure here could also include to a certain extent investment in fixed assets. On the other hand, some rural borrowers may lack working capital. Gaps in financial flows can arise due to the seasonal nature of the business, which is particularly the case for agricultural producers. At the same time, Figure 4.1- in the section on green financial products – shows that a significant share of loan takers use the money to switch livestock species and breeds and to buy new or alternative feed crop varieties. This could be considered as investments in "fixed" assets. One can assume the reality for rural respondents is likely a mixture of both reasons: borrowing for working capital and reinvesting the money to increase production.

Table 4.2. The rural population borrows to cover operational expenditure

Business (Investment in fixed assets, e.g. cars, facilities, buildings)	**16.9%**	6.8%
Business (Operational expenditure e.g. seeds, labour, material for production)	8.8%	**23.2%**

Source: OECD Kyrgyz Household Survey on Green Finance

Most respondents said they were satisfied with the service received. However, 42 respondents (18.6% of those who took out a loan) were dissatisfied because they felt interest rates were too high.

The more than 70% of respondents who had not taken out a loan mentioned different reasons for not having borrowed money. For most, interest rates were too high. (Respondents could choose multiple answers. Therefore, percentages were adjusted for the number of responses rather than total number of respondents). In other findings, 11% said they had not taken a loan because they had no bank account. Around 10% were afraid of corruption or bribes, which reflects the low trust in the financial system identified in Chapter 2. Another 9.5% said they did not need to borrow money because they had enough.

Most of the other reasons relate to access and use, ineligibility for loans or lack of understanding of the financial product. Around 9% mentioned the lending term was too short. Around 7% had trouble accessing and using banking services, which relates to the use of banking services explained above. Around 6% had insufficient collateral to pledge. For around 5%, the repayment schedule was inconvenient, while 4% lacked information about how they could use the loan. Around another 4% lacked information about financial products. Religion (around 1%) was not a major reason for why people did not take out a loan.

These findings suggest that financial products and services that do not meet the needs of potential users are the main reasons for not borrowing money. It does not suggest that most people would not be willing to take out a loan (except for those who said they have enough money or did not answer the question). Rather, the findings suggest that people have actively tried but were unsuccessful or deterred by the reasons shown in Figure 4.21.

Figure 4.21. Reasons for not taking out a loan

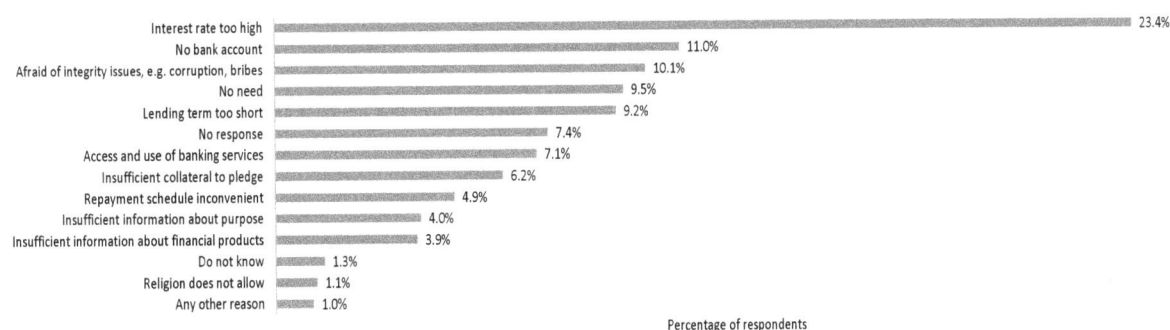

Note: Respondents were able to choose multiple answers.
Source: OECD Kyrgyz Household Survey on Green Finance

The reasons for not taking out a loan differ by oblast, but there is no clear trend across oblasts except for integrity issues, as shown in Table 4.3. Across all oblasts, integrity issues – defined here as people fearing corruption or bribes – are a strong deterrent for not taking out a loan.

Respondents in Talas ranked lack of bank account as the strongest barrier. In Batken, respondents ranked high interest rates as the biggest deterrent for not taking out a loan. Respondents in Naryn ranked short lending terms as the strongest barrier. In Osh and Osh city, respondents reported low levels of information on financial products as the primary reason they did not take out a loan. In Issy-Kul, respondents reported religion as the reason, together with fearing integrity issues, as a strong deterrent for not taking out a loan.

Table 4.3. Reasons for not taking out a loan, by oblast

Reasons for not taking out a loan	Bishkek city	Chui	Issyk-Kul	Naryn	Talas	Osh oblast	Jalal-Abad	Batken	Osh city
No need	20.3%	3.0%	1.5%	3.7%	0.0%	8.9%	12.5%	10.4%	4.1%
Afraid of integrity issues	11.7%	31.3%	25.4%	22.2%	31.3%	27.8%	16.3%	26.9%	22.4%
Interest rate too high	8.6%	10.8%	13.4%	7.4%	0.0%	8.4%	5.6%	17.2%	6.1%
No bank account	6.3%	3.0%	9.0%	0.0%	25.0%	4.6%	1.9%	12.7%	4.1%
Lending term too short	5.5%	9.0%	9.0%	22.2%	0.0%	4.2%	6.3%	2.2%	8.2%
Insufficient collateral to pledge	5.5%	1.2%	3.0%	3.7%	6.3%	2.1%	11.3%	.7%	10.2%
You have difficulties in understanding how to access and use the banking services.	4.7%	3.6%	0.0%	0.0%	0.0%	3.4%	10.0%	3.0%	8.2%
Insufficient information about financial products	2.3%	3.6%	0.0%	7.4%	0.0%	21.1%	8.8%	0.0%	24.5%
Religion	2.3%	15.7%	25.4%	7.4%	12.5%	3.8%	6.9%	0.0%	0.0%
Don't know	2.3%	1.2%	0.0%	0.0%	6.3%	.4%	1.9%	.7%	0.0%
Insufficient information about funding purpose	.8%	3.0%	1.5%	3.7%	0.0%	1.3%	0.0%	0.0%	0.0%
Repayment schedule inconvenient	0.0%	4.8%	6.0%	7.4%	18.8%	1.7%	7.5%	.7%	2.0%
No response	29.7%	5.4%	6.0%	11.1%	0.0%	11.8%	10.6%	25.4%	10.2%
Other reason	0.0%	4.2%	0.0%	3.7%	0.0%	.4%	.6%	0.0%	0.0%

Note: Respondents were able to choose multiple answers.
Source: OECD Kyrgyz Household Survey on Green Finance

More than 80% of respondents who took out loans were satisfied with the quality of the financial product and services. At the same time, 4.2% of respondents who took out a loan expressed dissatisfaction with the quality of the financial product due to the high borrowing rate.

References

Demirgüç-Kunt, A. et al. (2018), *The Global Findex Database 2017: Measuring Financial Inclusion and the Fintech Revolution*, (database), https://databank.worldbank.org/source/global-financial-inclusion (accessed on 12 February 2020). [3]

Hasanova, S. (2018), "Financial inclusion, financial regulation, financial literacy, and financial education in the Kyrgyz Republic", *Working Paper*, No. 850, Asian Development Bank Institute, Tokyo, https://www.adb.org/publications/financial-inclusion-regulation-literacy-education-kyrgyz-republic. [8]

Ministry for Education, Science & Culture of the Kyrgyz Republic (2000), *System of Education of Kyrgyzstan at present*, http://merope.bibl.u-szeged.hu/oseas/kyrgyz_system.html (accessed on 24 October 2020). [7]

National Statistical Committee of the Kyrgyz Republic (2020), *Сельское хозяйство Кыргызской Республики (Agriculture of the Kyrgyz Republic 2015-2019)*, National Statistical Committee of the Kyrgyz Republic, Bishkek, http://www.stat.kg/ru/publications/sbornik-selskoe-hozyajstvo-kyrgyzskoj-respubliki/. [1]

OECD (2019), *Roadmap for a National Strategy for Financial Education in Kyrgyz Republic*, https://www.oecd.org/education/financial-education-cis.htm. [5]

OECD/ILO (2017), *How Immigrants Contribute to Kyrgyzstan's Economy*, International Labour Organization, Geneva/OECD Publishing, Paris, https://dx.doi.org/10.1787/9789264287303-en. [6]

World Bank (2019), *Global Financial Development Database: October 2019 Version*, World Bank, Washington, DC, https://www.worldbank.org/en/publication/gfdr/data/global-financial-development-database (accessed on 11 February 2020). [4]

World Bank Group (2020), *Domestic Credit to Private Sector by Banks (% of GDP)*, (database), https://data.worldbank.org/indicator/FD.AST.PRVT.GD.ZS (accessed on 16 June 2020). [9]

Yamano, T. et al. (2019), *Kyrgyz Republic: Improving Growth Potential*, Asian Development Bank, Mandaluyong City, The Philippines, https://www.adb.org/publications/kyrgyz-republic-improving-growth-potential. [2]

Note

[1] Higher education is offered by academies, universities, institutes and colleges and is itself segmented into three levels: incomplete higher education, basic higher education (Bachelor degree and speciality) and complete higher education (Master's degree and speciality teaching) (Ministry for Education, Science & Culture of the Kyrgyz Republic, 2000[7])

5 Implications and policy recommendations

This chapter suggests interventions that can help improve access to and use of green financial products and services in the Kyrgyz Republic. Policy can play a role in making green investments more attractive. The central bank can consider mandatory requirements for financial institutions to improve their environmental governance, such as adequate pricing and disclosure of climate risks. Several other interventions are outlined, such as subsidies for climate and disaster risk insurance and information on green financial instruments within Kyrgyz financial literacy strategies. The chapter also presents options to provide long-term risk capital and alleviate collateral constraints through scaling up credit guarantees. This would especially help those household members that are individual entrepreneurs.

Overview

This report aimed to analyse the demand for and use of green financial instruments. The results clearly show that improving access to and use of green financial products and services needs to go hand in hand with efforts to increase the use of formal financial instruments in general. A functioning financial market where households and businesses actively use financial products and services is in many ways a precondition for introducing elements of green finance.

At the same time, the general policy framework can support the attractiveness of investing in green financial instruments for both households and industry. Such policies include setting tariffs for green electricity generation, lowering interest rates for energy efficiency improvements of homes or offering state-supported loans and similar instruments. These policies can lower some of the financial barriers of undertaking green investments for households.

In addition, financial and social inclusion as well as green finance are interlinked and mutually reinforce each other. A coherent legal and regulatory framework that targets the three issues is an important instrument.

The National Bank and the Government of Kyrgyzstan can increase the use of (green) banking products and services in several ways. These include supporting awareness and understanding among the population; subsidising access to tools such as disaster risk insurance; lowering collateral requirements; and allowing movable asset-based lending together with policies that are conducive to low-carbon, climate resilient investments.

The following sections outline interventions to improve access to and use of green financial products and services. Some instruments will help increase use of financial instruments in general, not just those that are green.

An effective regulatory framework

Kyrgyzstan should consider developing a green finance roadmap to set out its strategy on how to make the financial system more sustainable and connect financial flows to sustainability. Such a roadmap can build on the actions outlined in the Kyrgyz Green Economy Program. The Kyrgyz Ministry of Finance together with the National Bank and other relevant state entities that work on sustainability could lead the development of the strategy. In one key task, the government is to ensure that state entities collaborate to direct finance to sustainable projects through coherent policy. Another key task is to develop a vision that both public institutions and private actors can share.

As part of the roadmap, the National Bank of the Kyrgyz Republic can consider mandatory requirements to improve environmental, social and governance (ESG) principles in the operation of banks. Any such requirements would need to lead to wider and faster implementation of green finance activities among banking institutions compared to voluntary commitments. It is questionable whether non-regulatory instruments provide enough incentives for banks to develop products and services which they have not yet considered to date.

The regulatory environment is moving towards mandatory requirements, driven by the EU's Technical Expert Group on Sustainable Finance but also by efforts outside the European Union. The National Bank of Georgia, for example, launched a new set of principles in February 2020. These principles, developed by the OECD, aim to guide commercial banks on how to disclose and report on their ESG activities. The principles became mandatory in 2021. Ultimately, they will help increase transparency on ESG issues and improve market discipline as an important prerequisite for sustainable financing. It is worth investigating what Kyrgyzstan could take from the Georgian experience.

Offering more diverse and better targeted financial products

The survey shows that 5.5% of survey respondents would be interested in taking out agricultural or other disaster risk insurance and that 6% have done so. Financial products to manage risks such as insurance are important complements to credits and savings. A large proportion of smallholder farmers in the agricultural sector may not have large financial buffers in case of income losses. In addition, large areas of the country are vulnerable to the impacts of human-made climate change. Consequently, it is important to expand access to insurance in Kyrgyzstan.

The Kyrgyz government should consider incentives for setting up agricultural insurance systems to spark more development in the insurance market. Insurance providers have so far played a small role in the Kyrgyz economy (OECD, 2019[1]; Hasanova, 2018[2]). Subscribing to insurance would allow farmers to protect themselves against high fluctuations in their earnings and improve their credit standing. This, in turn, would enable small farmers especially to invest in modernising their farms, for example. The government could give some financial support for insurance payments (or benefits or payouts) to farmers. The government of Armenia, for example, introduced agricultural insurance schemes in 2019. A mix of domestic sources (from the Ministry of Agriculture), bilateral and international funding (from KfW Development Bank and the Climate Investment Fund) will subsidise insurance payments up to 60% to cover agricultural losses from weather-related events (Agroinsurance, 2019[3]).

The survey also sheds light on where Kyrgyz households need more information and support for green financial instruments. Almost 35% wish for support to lower interest rates and around the same number wish for more patient capital and more lenient repayment schedules so they can use a green financial product. Data from the National Bank of the Kyrgyz Republic confirm that interest rates on loans are high. Average weighted interest rates on loans from commercial banks for private consumers were 24% in 2019 (13% on mortgages) (National Bank of the Kyrgyz Republic, 2020[4]). Weighted interest rates on loans from microfinance institutions for private consumers were 32% in 2019 on average (30% on mortgages and construction) (National Bank of the Kyrgyz Republic, 2020[4]). If institutions had more information on borrowers' credit history, credit risk decreases and financial institutions could lower interest rates for some clients. This idea was explored in Chapter 2, in the section titled "Overcoming challenges in the banking sector".

More flexibility in the approach to collateral could also make it easier for potential loan takers to receive credit. Collaterals are assets that a lender accepts as security for a loan. In the survey, lack of sufficient collateral, although not the highest barrier, was still a stumbling block for respondents who wanted a loan or green loan. In all, 6.5% wished for more support to fulfil collateral requirements, while 10% mentioned that insufficient collateral poses a hypothetical barrier to using a green financial product.

Small enterprises in Kyrgyzstan in particular struggle with high collateral requirements (OECD, 2018[5]; Hasanova, 2018[2]). Collateral requirements imposed by the central bank are relatively high. They demand collateral of at least 120% of the loan amount (OECD, 2018[6]). This is the minimum amount, however; collateral requirements demanded by commercial banks can be higher (OECD, 2018[6]). In fact, the average value of collateral needed for a loan in the Kyrgyz Republic amounted to almost 300% of the loan amount for small enterprises in 2019 and more than 90% of business loans require collateral (World Bank, 2020[7]). The challenge of valuation issues is particularly acute for SMEs in the agriculture sector. This is especially true for those in the south because of their assets in remote, rural areas (OECD, 2018[6]).

The International Finance Corporation (IFC) has started to promote movable asset-based lending to allow smaller businesses to use assets like machinery and crops as collateral for loans (Development Partners' Coordination Council, 2016[8]). Outcomes from this project should be evaluated. If positive, outcomes should be used to trial movable asset-based lending across commercial banks and microfinance institutions. It could also be considered whether to extend this measure to households. In addition, the

National Bank could consider decreasing minimum collateral requirements given that collateral requirements are much higher in reality.

A credit guarantee fund has been set up to alleviate collateral constraints for businesses. If a business fails to fulfil collateral requirements of a commercial bank, it can apply for a guarantee from the Guarantee Fund. Since its establishment in 2016, the fund has provided more than 2 000 guarantees amounting to more than KGS 2 billion (USD 24 million) (OECD, 2018[9]). As of 2020, the amount of loans issued by banks under the guarantees exceeds KGS 7 billion (USD 80 million) (OECD, 2018[9]). SMEs have received 90% (OECD, 2018[9]). In May 2020, the National Bank of the Kyrgyz Republic added KGS 1 billion KGS (USD 12 million) to the authorised capital of the fund to help SMEs weather the COVID-19 pandemic (OECD, 2018[9]). Further increasing the size of the fund over the coming years could help make a significant difference in access to credit, particularly for individual entrepreneurs. Only around 17% of small enterprises (under 20 employees) had a bank loan or line of credit in 2019 compared to 40% of large (more than 100 employees) and 35% medium-sized (between 20-100 employees) enterprises (World Bank, 2020[7]).

Financing opportunities are also limited by the lack of breadth of financial products, particularly risk capital (OECD, 2018[6]). Although this is more relevant for business owners than households, new products could help mitigate financing constraints for SMEs, including individual entrepreneurs. The Highland Private Equity and Mezzanine Fund (OECD, 2018[6]) is trying to address this gap. The fund, set up in 2014, aims to provide long-term risk capital to SMEs (OECD, 2018[10]). Positive examples from its investments can help expand private equity and mezzanine finance as an asset class in the Kyrgyz Republic. According to the fund, it tries to operate according to its own ESG policy (Highland Capital, 2020[11]) and could thus help promote green investment activities.

Tapping into remittance flows is another area that can be used to motivate more households to bring additional money into the financial sector. More than 10% of the Kyrgyz population work in the Russian Federation and the money they send back accounts for a third of gross domestic product (Fitzgeorge-Parker, 2018[12]). According to Hasanova (2018[2]), the population only reluctantly bring remittances to the financial sector and most banks lack special financial products for them. Migrants send money via money transfer services without opening an account, and their families receive cash (Hasanova, 2018[2]). The receiving households use most of the additional money to cover current consumption, to invest in durable goods such as housing and cars or, especially in rural areas, to invest in livestock [Lukashova and Makenbaeva cited in (Hasanova, 2018[2]); (OECD, 2018[13])]. Although investment in physical capital and durable consumption contribute to well-being, other types of investments such as in human capital (e.g. education) or financial capital is important for long-run development (Kroeger and Anderson, 2014[14]). Data show that remittance flows in Kyrgyzstan are not contributing to such development (Kroeger and Anderson, 2014[14]; OECD, 2018[13]; Muktarbek kyzy, Seyitov and Jenish, 2015[15]).

Only some banks try to attract this money by explaining to migrants' families the advantages of opening an account and offering different kinds of deposits in national currency or Russian roubles (Hasanova, 2018[2]). Banks could introduce special services and products for migrants more widely. They can make transfer systems cheaper, more accessible and more transparent. They can also help customers combine remittance accounts with other financial products.

Increasing awareness and understanding of green financial products and services

The study has shown that Kyrgyz households have some experience with financial products. Their awareness of green financial products, however, is lacking or limited. The follow-up strategy to the Program to Improve Financial Literacy in the Kyrgyz Republic for 2016-2020 could include a focus on green finance.

This could detail measures and activities on how to further increase financial literacy and awareness of green financial products, as well as action plans to monitor and assess implementation.

Financial institutions could offer training on green finance to their front-line staff to help potential clients become more aware of the purpose of green loans and green investments in general. The Green Economy Program of the Kyrgyz Republic 2019-2023 outlines steps to promote sustainable finance. It already includes the goal to train employees and customers of Kyrgyz commercial banks and microfinance institutions on sustainable finance. The Union of Banks of Kyrgyzstan together with IFC will start to promote that financial institutions integrate ESG principles into their risk assessment and financial decision making in Kyrgyzstan from 2021. They will also try to increase awareness on green finance among financial service providers.

The National Bank of the Kyrgyz Republic and relevant public, private and civil society stakeholders can embed a focus on green financial products and services within general efforts to increase financial literacy. This can help increase both financial literacy and awareness of green finance instruments. The National Bank and other institutions involved in financial education could also consider joining the OECD International Network on Financial Education. Members of the network from over 130 economies work on key policy areas related to financial education such as standard setting, implementation and evaluation and the impact of digitalisation (OECD, 2020[16]). Meanwhile, the Network for Greening the Financial System, as well as the Sustainable Banking Network, provide platforms for peer-to-peer learning. Working together, members define and promote best practices on how the financial system can manage risks and mobilise capital for green investments.

References

Agroinsurance (2019), "Armenia: Govt approved the procedure for subsidizing insurance payments under the pilot ag insurance program", 25 October, Agroinsurance, https://agroinsurance.com/en/armenia-govt-approved-the-procedure-for-subsidizing-insurance-payments-under-the-pilot-ag-insurance-program/. [3]

Development Partners' Coordination Council (2016), "World Bank Group helps improve Kyrgyz Republic's financial infrastructure", Press Release, 27 June, Development Partners' Coordination Council, http://www.donors.kg/en/2816-world-bank-group-helps-improve-kyrgyz-republic-s-financial-infrastructure (accessed on 6 March 2020). [8]

Fitzgeorge-Parker, L. (2018), "Impact Banking: Microfinance Comes of Age in Kyrgyzstan", webpage, https://www.euromoney.com/article/b1b0967crmxs3m/impact-banking-microfinance-comes-of-age-in-kyrgyzstan?copyrightInfo=true (accessed on 8 March 2020). [12]

Hasanova, S. (2018), "Financial inclusion, financial regulation, financial literacy, and financial education in the Kyrgyz Republic", Working Paper, No. 850, Asian Development Bank Institute, Tokyo, https://www.adb.org/publications/financial-inclusion-regulation-literacy-education-kyrgyz-republic. [2]

Highland Capital (2020), About Us, webpage, https://highland.kg/ (accessed on 16 October 2020). [11]

Kroeger, A. and K. Anderson (2014), "Remittances and the human capital of children: New evidence from Kyrgyzstan during revolution and financial crisis, 2005–2009", Journal of Comparative Economics, Vol. 42/3, pp. 770-785, https://doi.org/10.1016/j.jce.2013.06.001. [14]

Muktarbek kyzy, A., T. Seyitov and N. Jenish (2015), *Remittances and Expenditure Patterns of Households in the Kyrgyz Republic*, Economic Research Center of the National Bank of the Kyrgyz Republic, Bishkek, https://www.nbkr.kg/DOC/12022016/000000000040456.pdf.   [15]

National Bank of the Kyrgyz Republic (2020), *Bulletin of the National Bank of the Kyrgyz Republic*, No. 9, National Bank of the Kyrgyz Republic, Bishkek, https://www.nbkr.kg/index1.jsp?item=137&lang=ENG.   [4]

OECD (2020), "OECD International Network on Financial Education", webpage, https://www.oecd.org/financial/education/oecd-international-network-on-financial-education.htm (accessed on xx xx 2021).   [16]

OECD (2019), *Roadmap for a National Strategy for Financial Education in Kyrgyz Republic*, https://www.oecd.org/education/financial-education-cis.htm.   [1]

OECD (2018), "Business environment in Central Asia: Access to finance", in *Enhancing Competitiveness in Central Asia*, OECD Publishing, Paris, https://dx.doi.org/10.1787/9789264288133-5-en.   [5]

OECD (2018), "Business environment in Central Asia: Access to finance", in *Enhancing Competitiveness in Central Asia*, OECD Publishing, Paris, https://dx.doi.org/10.1787/9789264288133-5-en.   [6]

OECD (2018), "Business environment in Central Asia: Access to finance", in *Enhancing Competitiveness in Central Asia*, OECD Publishing, Paris, https://dx.doi.org/10.1787/9789264288133-5-en.   [9]

OECD (2018), "Business environment in Central Asia: Access to finance", in *Enhancing Competitiveness in Central Asia*, OECD Publishing, Paris, https://dx.doi.org/10.1787/9789264288133-5-en.   [10]

OECD (2018), "Business environment in Central Asia: Access to finance", in *Enhancing Competitiveness in Central Asia*, OECD Publishing, Paris, https://dx.doi.org/10.1787/9789264288133-5-en.   [13]

World Bank (2020), *Enterprise Surveys*, (database), http://www.enterprisesurveys.org (accessed on 2 August 2020).   [7]

Annex A. Survey method and implementation

Households were selected using sequential random sampling, which consists of the following stages:

- Households are selected by means of random numbers associated with serial numbers of households in the list.
- Households already selected cannot be selected again.
- Households are selected and interviewed strictly according to the order of generating the random numbers.
- Households, which failed to be interviewed (not found, refusal, etc.), are replaced with the next ones, according to the order of the random numbers.
- Selection is repeated until a required number of interviews is reached.

Interviewers used the Kish grids to select respondents at household level. The interviewers had a Visit Registration Form and a Respondent Selection form together with each questionnaire. The procedure of selection of respondents consisted of the following stages:

- All household members eligible for the survey (aged 18-64) were sorted by gender (primary sorting key) and then by age (secondary key).
- Each of them was assigned a serial number.
- A respondent was determined according to the Kish grid.
- If the determined respondent was not eligible by quota, the next household member was chosen for the survey.

In general, respondents had no trouble understanding the questions in the questionnaire. Interviewers, however, faced several issues while carrying out the interviews:

- Some of the respondents refused to take part in the survey. Reasons included:
  - Respondents were busy and had no time for answering questions.
  - Questions devoted to credits and loans made many respondents feel uncomfortable and caused aggression and unwillingness to answer the questions, especially in the southern parts of Kyrgyzstan.
  - Some respondents showed disinterest in green economy and sustainable development.
  - Some respondents refused to give a phone number for security reasons.
- The presence of heavy doors, surveillance cameras and fences in Bishkek made it difficult for interviewers to physically access households. Moreover, in many parts of Bishkek, warnings about frequent thefts and attacks are posted at the entrance doors of the porches. They ask people not to open the door to strangers. Interviewers had to find the house committee and explain to them about the survey and its purposes.
- Due to the arrest of Kyrgyzstan's former president, political instability occurred during the fieldwork stage. This created life-threatening and therefore unfavourable survey conditions in Bishkek and the Chui region.
- During the fieldwork, local people had conflict with Chinese workers in Solton Sary. This caused dangerous and unfavourable conditions for survey conditions in the Naryn region.

Household access to banking facilities varies depending on where people live in Kyrgyzstan (rural or urban settings). Therefore, the survey makes an important contribution to represent the geographic distribution of the population (Annex B further elaborates this point). The survey has, however, several limitations.

First, the survey excludes people under the age of 18. While there are legal reasons for this, the population under 18 makes up more than one-third of the population (National Statistical Committee of the Kyrgyz Republic, 2019[1]). Results might look different if the population between 16 and 18, who are allowed to earn money, had been included in the study. In particular, results on use of mobile banking might look different.

Second, someone within the household might have a bank account or have taken out a loan, but the respondent may have interviewed another household member. The survey design did not take this into account. This should be kept in mind when interpreting results on use of bank accounts.

Third, socio-economic characteristics such as income or type of occupation were not included in the quota to select respondents. Readers should therefore not interpret these as representative of the national population.

Lastly, this report has focused on households. To some extent, household finances are closely interlinked with those of small business holders and individual entrepreneurs. Findings on financial literacy, services and products will have some predictive power for Kyrgyz firms and potentially a higher degree of precision compared to sampling firms. Nevertheless, the sample only captures issues related to the business environment to a limited extent.

The data gathered here, despite their limitations, make an important contribution to the empirical evidence on access to financial products and services and their use in Kyrgyzstan.

Annex B. Demographic characteristics of the sample

The following section describes the survey sample and its demographic characteristics.

The gender distribution is roughly equal between respondents who identify as female (50.7%) and male (49.3%) among the sample population, i.e. the part of the population that took part in the household survey.

The survey is representative of the age distribution among the population living in Kyrgyzstan aged between 18-64 (Figure A B.1).

Figure A B.1. Age distribution among respondents, in percentage

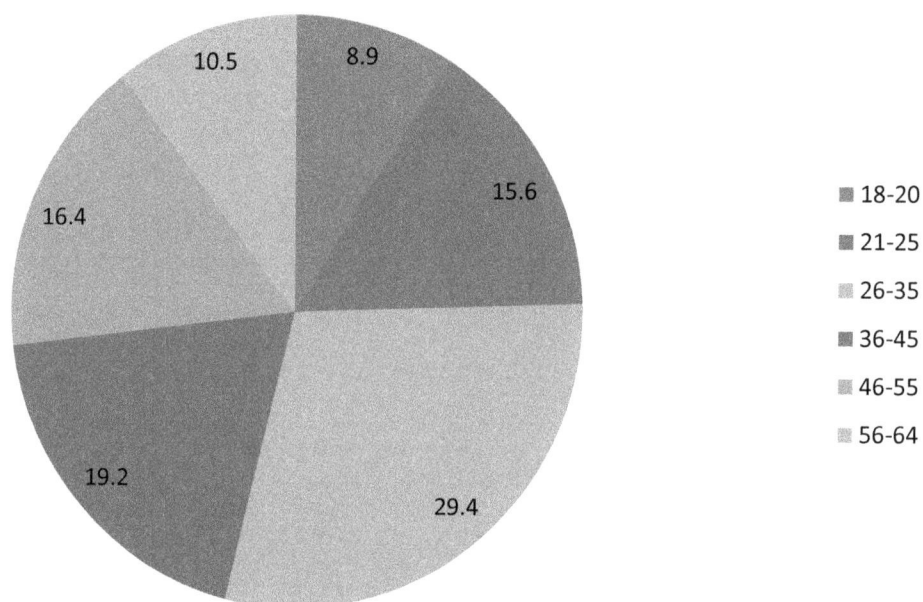

Source: OECD Kyrgyz Household Survey on Green Finance

They break down as follows: almost 30% of respondents are between 26-35 years-old and then roughly equally distributed among age groups from 21-25 years-old, 36-45 years-old and 46-55 years-old. The smallest segments are respondents aged 56-64 and 18-20, both making up roughly 10% of respondents.

Figure A B.2. Household size by number of people, in percentage

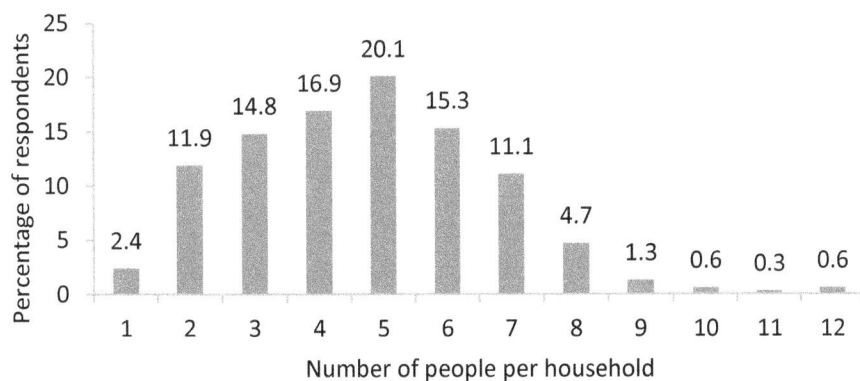

Source: OECD Kyrgyz Household Survey on Green Finance

Most respondents have up to five members in their household (Figure A B.1).

Figure A B.3. Respondents' marital status

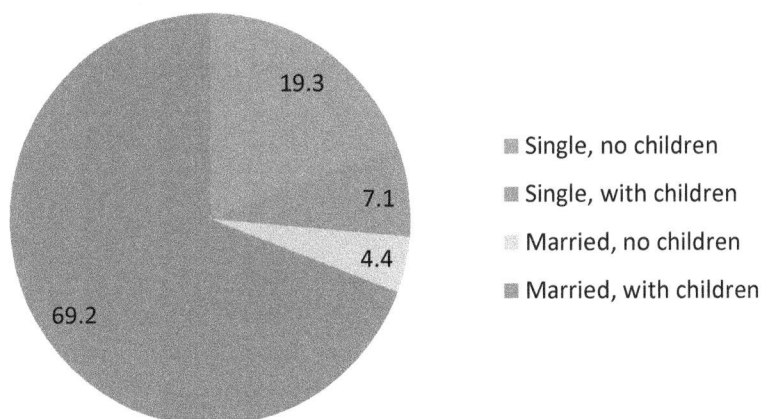

Source: OECD Kyrgyz Household Survey on Green Finance

Most (around 70% of respondents) are married with children (Figure A B.3). In addition, around 4% are married without children, around 7% are single parents and around 19% are single and do not have children.

Figure A B.4. Education level of respondents

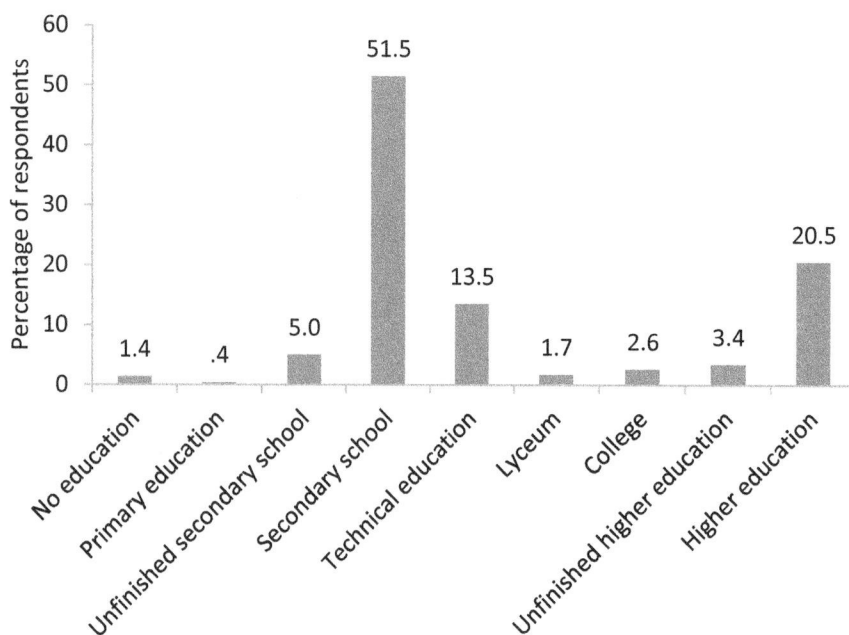

Source: OECD Kyrgyz Household Survey on Green Finance

Most people have attained education levels up to secondary education and a fifth of respondents have gone through higher education (Figure A B.4).

Figure A B.5. Respondents' monthly income

In KGS

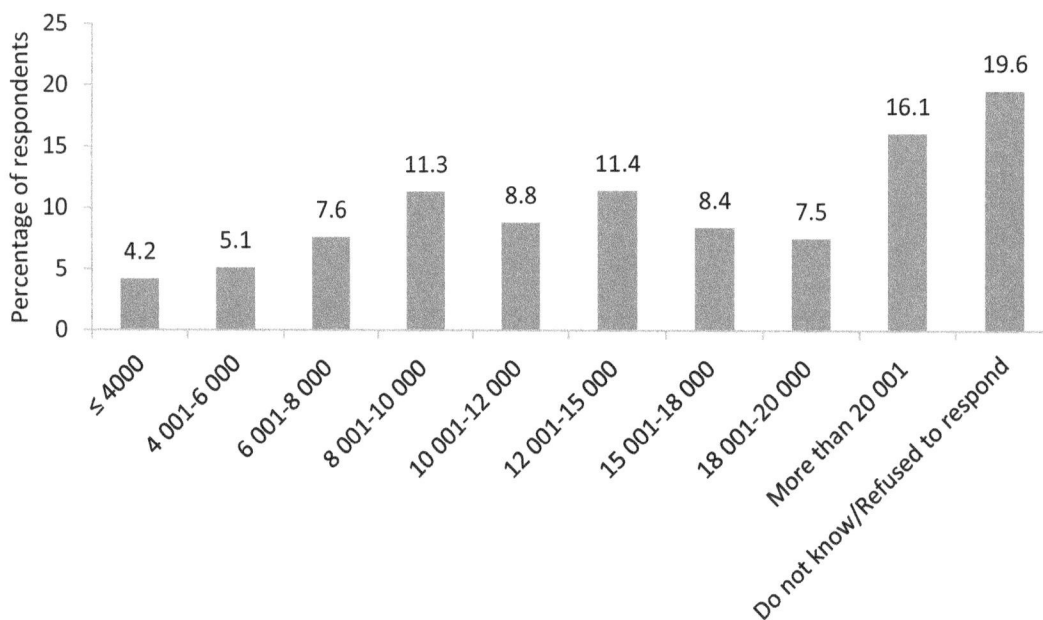

Source: OECD Kyrgyz Household Survey on Green Finance

Figure A B.5 shows the distribution of monthly income levels among respondents. In all, around 36% responded that they earned between KGS 10 000-20 000 per month. Around 30% earn less than KGS 10 000. Only a small percentage of respondents (around 4%) earn less than KGS 4 000. Around 16% of respondents earn more than KGS 20 000 per month. On average, respondents dispose of a monthly income amounting to around KGS 16 000 (depending on which value sets the category of "more than 20 001"). Median income for respondents lies at KGS 16 500. The income of respondents is therefore roughly comparable to the average monthly income per capita in Kyrgyzstan (KGS 16 427 in 2018) (National Statistical Committee of the Kyrgyz Republic, n.d.[2]). Nevertheless, the different income brackets should not be interpreted as being representative of the national population.

Figure A B.6. Employment status, in percentage

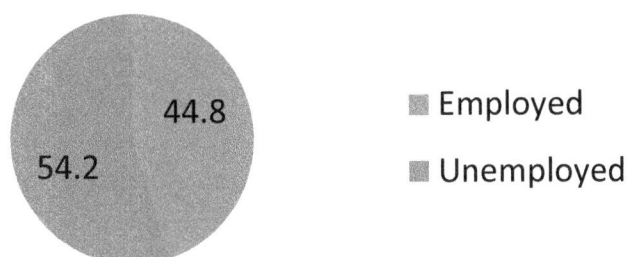

Source: OECD Kyrgyz Household Survey on Green Finance

As shown in Figure A B.6, over half respondents are not employed. Of those who are unemployed as shown in Figure A B.7, most are homemakers or on parental leave (32%), almost 23% are looking for employment and around 16% are not looking for employment. Around 15% of respondents are retired and around 10% are students.

Figure A B.7. Reasons given for being unemployed, in percentage

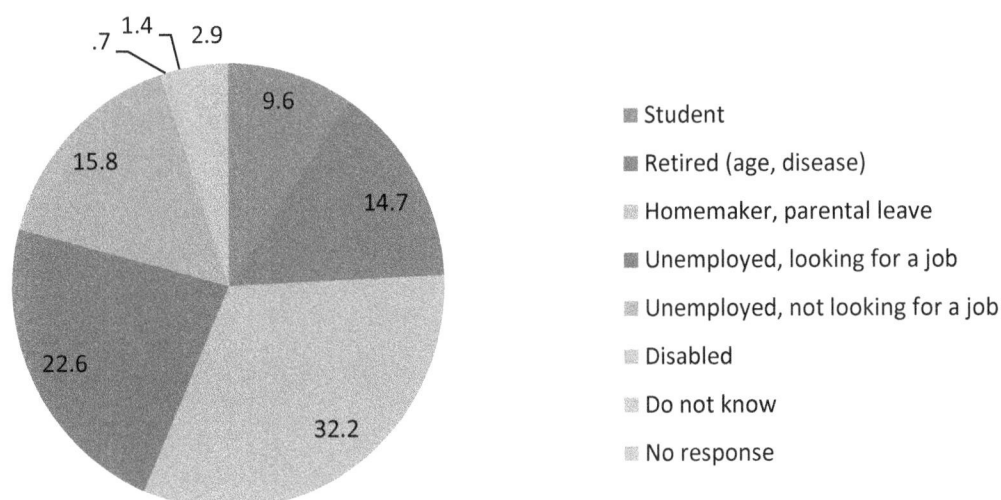

Source: OECD Kyrgyz Household Survey on Green Finance

Figure A B.8. Sector of employment, in percentage

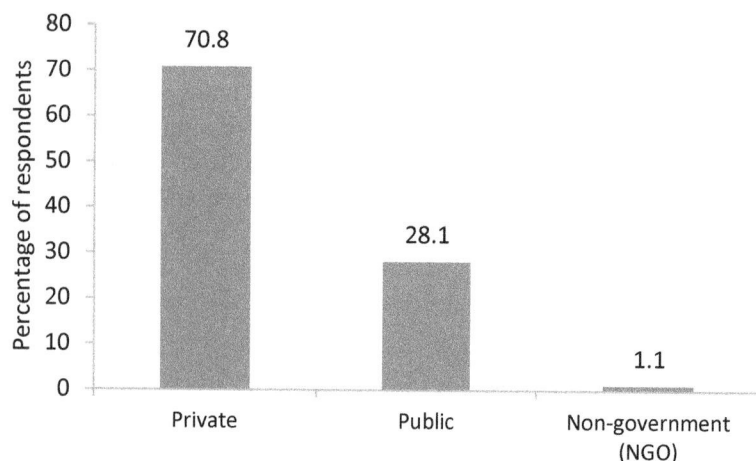

Of the around 45% of people who are employed, more than 70% work in the private sector, around 30% in the public sector and around 1% work for non-governmental organisations (Figure A B.8).

Figure A B.9. Type of employment, in percentage

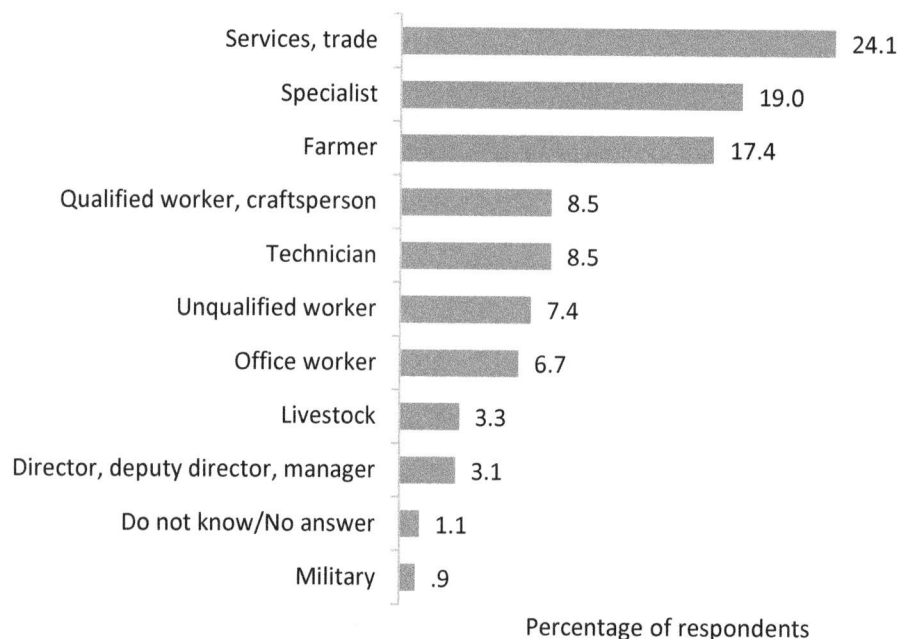

More specifically, of the around 45% of people who are employed Of the around 45% of people who are employed, more than 70% work in the private sector, around 30% in the public sector and around 1% work for non-governmental organisations (Figure A B.8).

Figure A B.9 shows that almost a quarter of respondents work in the services and/or trade sector, followed by specialists in a particular type of work (19%) and farmers (around 17%).

Figure A B.10 presents additional categories of the specific types of sectors or occupations of respondents.

Figure A B.10. Type of sector, in percentage

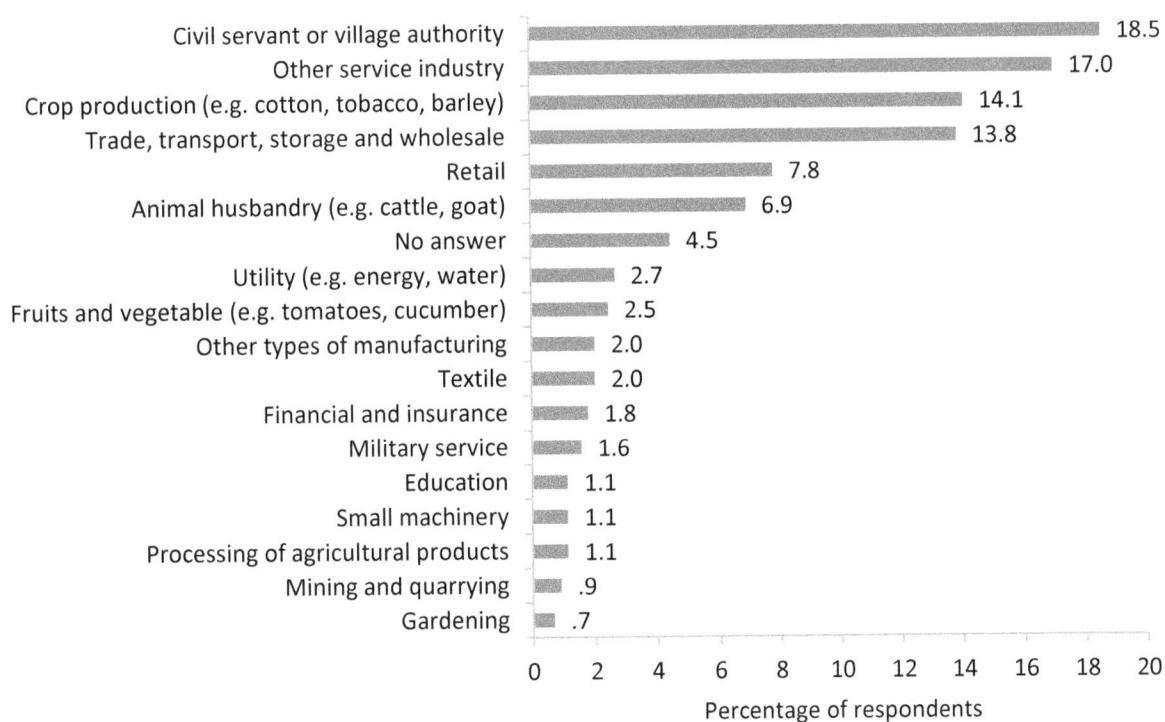

Source: OECD Kyrgyz Household Survey on Green Finance

The survey covers the regions of Kyrgyzstan. The regional distribution of the sample population is representative of where people live (Figure A B.12). This includes both the distribution across oblasts and across rural and urban areas. The sample is representative of the distribution of the population in rural and urban areas. The country is divided into seven regions or *oblasts* and Bishkek and Osh form two independent cities. According to estimates from 2015, the oblasts Osh and Jalal-Abad together with the capital Bishkek are the most populated oblasts (EIU Country Analysis, 2019[3]). Accordingly, most respondents are based in these regions (Figure A B.12). At the same time, more than 60% of respondents live in rural areas, as shown in Figure A B.11.

Figure A B.11. Distribution of respondents by type of settlement, in percentage

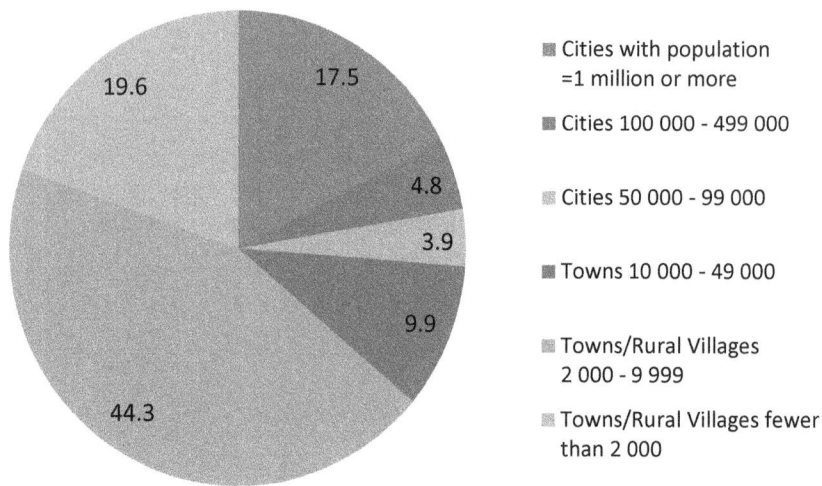

Source: OECD Kyrgyz Household Survey on Green Finance

Figure A B.12. Regional distribution of respondents by oblast, in percentage

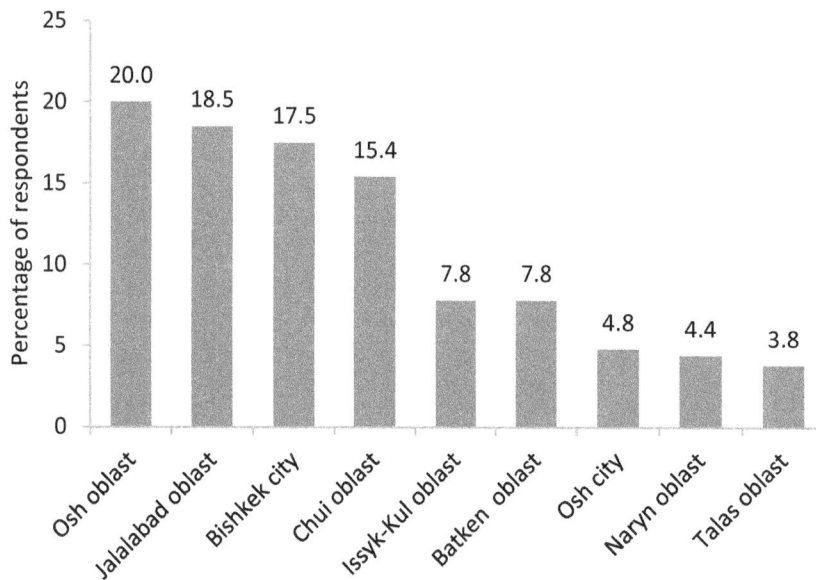

Source: OECD Kyrgyz Household Survey on Green Finance

Table A B.1. Regional distribution of survey respondents in total numbers

Oblast	Number of questionnaires
Batken region	78
Jalal-Abad region	185
Isyk-Kul region	78
Naryn region	44
Osh region	200
Talas region	38
Chuy area	154
Bishkek	175
Osh city	48
TOTAL:	**1 000**

Source: OECD Kyrgyz Household Survey on Green Finance

Annex C. Survey questionnaire in English

General information about the respondent

1. Gender of respondent (Single answer)
    1. Male
    2. Female

2. Age of respondent, years (Single answer)
    1. 18-20
    2. 21-25
    3. 26-35
    4. 36-45
    5. 46-55
    6. 56-64
    7. 65 and over

3. What is your educational background?

No education	1	College	7
Primary education	2	Unfinished higher education	8
Unfinished secondary school	3	Higher education	9
Secondary school	4	Academic degree (e.g. graduate or doctoral degree)	10
Technical education	5	Don't know	98
Lyceum	6	Refused to respond	99

4. What is your marital/family status?
    1. Single, no children
    2. Single, with children
    3. Married, no children
    4. Married, with children

5. What is the monthly income of your household (in KGSs)? Please count all net incomes, including salaries, pensions, grants, etc.

Up to 700 KGS	1	6 001-8 000 KGS	9
701-900 KGS	2	8 001-10 000 KGS	10
901-1 200 KGS	3	10 01-12 000 KGS	11
1 201-1 500 KGS	4	12 001-15 000 KGS	12
1 501-2 000 KGS	5	15 001-18 000 KGS	13
2 001-3 000 KGS	6	18 001-20 000 KGS	14
3 001-4 000 KGS	7	More than 20 001 KGS	15
4 001-6 000 KGS	8	Don't know/Refused to respond	99

6. How many people are there in your household, including you?

7. Are you currently employed?

Yes	1	Skip to Q9
No	2	Skip to Q8
Don't know	98	Then to Q12
No response	99	

8. If you are not employed, what is your status?

Student	1	Unemployed, not looking for a job	5
Retired (age, disease)	2	Other _____	6
Home maker, parental leave	3	Don't know	98
Unemployed, looking for a job	4	No response	99

Please skip to Q12.

9. Which sector do you work in – private, public or non-government (NGO)?

Private	1	Non-government (NGO)	3
Public	2	Don't know/No answer	99

10. What is your current occupation?

Director, deputy director, manager	1	Unqualified worker	7
Specialist	2	Farmer	8
Technician	3	Military	9
Office worker	4	Other_____	10
Services, trade	5	Don't know/No answer	99
Qualified worker, craftsperson	6		

11. What is the economic activity that is the most relevant to your occupation? (Single answer)

1. Crop production (e.g. cotton, tobacco, barley, sugar beet, lucerne seeds, seed potatoes)
2. Fruits and vegetable sector (e.g. tomatoes, cucumber, cherry tomatoes, berries, cherry, fresh beans, medicinal herbs)
3. Animal husbandry (e.g. cattle, goat and sheep breeding)
4. Poultry and egg production
5. Gardening
6. Processing of agricultural products
7. Textile
8. Small machinery
9. Other types of manufacturing industry
10. Mining and quarrying
11. Trade, transport, storage and wholesale
12. Retail
13. Utility (e.g. energy, water, heat supplies)
14. Financial and insurance
15. Other service industry
16. Civil servant or municipal worker (e.g. aiyl okmotu)
17. Scientific research
18. Military service
19. Unemployed
20. No answer

12. Types of settlements (Single answer)

1. Cities with population = 1 million or more
2. Cities 500 000 - 999 000
3. Cities 100 000 - 499 000
4. Cities 50 000 - 99 000
5. Towns 10 000 - 49 000
6. Towns/Rural Villages 2 000 - 9 999
7. Towns/Rural Villages fewer than 2 000

13. Which city/oblast do you live in? (Single answer)

	CIRCLE ONE RESPONSE:
Bishkek city	1
Chuiskaya oblast	2
Talasskaya oblast	3
Narynskaya oblast	4
Issyk-Kulskaya oblast	5
Osh city	6
Oshskaya oblast	7
Jalalabatskaya oblast	8
Batkenskaya oblast	9

Questions about the subject

14. Do you have a bank account? (Single answer)

Yes	1	Skip to Q15
No	2	Skip to Q16
Don't know	98	
No response	99	

15. Do you use mobile banking?

Yes	1
No	2
Don't know	98
No response	99

16. Over the past 5 years, have you taken a loan or any other form of financial product from a bank or a non-bank financial institution <u>for any reasons</u>? Please circle the number in each of the columns "a" to "c".

	a. Banks	b. Microfinance institutions/ Microcredit organizations	c. Credit Unions
Yes, but only once	1	4	7
Yes, repeatedly	2	5	8
No	3	6	9

17. If your answer to Question 16 is YES, what was the amount of money you took? (If you have held multiple loans or other financial products, please indicate the amount <u>on average per loan/product</u>.) (Single answer)

If your question to Question 16 <u>is NO</u>, please skip to Question 19.

1. Up to USD 500 (Up to KGS 35 000)
2. USD 501 to USD 1 000 (KGS 35 001 to KGS 70 000)
3. USD 1 001 to USD 2 000 (KGS 70 001 to KGS 140 000)
4. USD 2 001 to USD 5 000 (KGS 140 001 to KGS 350 000)
5. USD 5 001 to USD 10 000 (KGS 350 001 to KGS 700 000)

6. USD 10 001 to USD 50 000 (KGS 700 001 to KGS 3 500 000)

7. More than USD 50 000 (More than KGS 3 500 000)

8. Don't know

9. No response

18. If your answer to Question 16 is YES, what was your main purpose (or purposes) for borrowing money? (Multiple choice)

1. Personal (mortgage / housing)

2. Personal (other purposes)

3. Business (Investment in fixed assets, e.g. cars, facilities, buildings, etc.)

4. Business (operation expenditure e.g. seeds, labour, material for production, etc.)

5. Repayment of debts

6. Don't know

7. No response

19. If your answer to Question 16 is NO, what is the main reason(s)? (multiple choice)

1. You do not have a bank account.

2. You have difficulties in understanding how to access and use the banking services.

3. Interest rate is too high.

4. Lending term is too short.

5. Repayment schedule is not convenient enough.

6. You do not have sufficient collateral to pledge.

7. You do not have enough information about financial products to make a good decision.

8. You do not have enough information about activities for which the funding should be used.

9. You would be afraid of integrity issues such as corruption and bribes.

10. Any other reason (Please specify)_____

11. Don't know

12. No response

20. [Please answer this question, if your answer to Question 16 is YES.]

Over the past 5 years, have you taken loans or any other form of financial products from a bank or non-bank financial institution to purchase equipment for any of the following activities? (Multiple choice)

1.	Production of energy from renewable sources (e.g. solar panels, biogas plants)	Y/N
2.	Electricity/heat/energy saving and management (e.g. house insulation, more efficient boilers)	Y/N
3.	Management of water use (e.g. more efficient irrigation systems, better access to clean water, etc.)	Y/N
4.	Wastewater management	Y/N
5.	Waste management	Y/N
6.	Switching crops to the ones that are more environmentally-friendly or resilient to changing climate/weather	Y/N
7.	Switching choice of livestock species and breeds	Y/N
8.	Use of new and alternative feed crop varieties for livestock	Y/N
9.	Protection of biodiversity and landscapes	Y/N
10.	Management of forest resources (e.g. agro-forestry, wildfire reduction, etc.)	Y/N
11.	Protection of ambient air (avoiding outdoor air pollution)	Y/N
12.	Agriculture insurance or any other disaster risk insurance	Y/N
13.	Any other activity (Please specify what the activity is.) _____	Y/N
14.	Don't know	Y
15.	No response	Y

21. If your answer to Question 20 is YES, what was the amount of money you took? (If you have held multiple loans or other financial products, please indicate the amount on average per loan/product.) (Single answer)

1. Up to USD 500 (Up to KGS 35 000)
2. USD 501 to USD 1 000 (KGS 35 001 to KGS 70 000)
3. USD 1 001 to USD 2 000 (KGS 70 001 to KGS 140 000)
4. USD 2 001 to USD 5 000 (KGS 140 001 to KGS 350 000)
5. USD 5 001 to USD 10 000 (KGS 350 001 to KGS 700 000)
6. USD 10 001 to USD 50 000 (KGS 700 001 to KGS 3 500 000)
7. More than USD 50 000 (More than KGS 3 500 000)
8. Don't know
9. No response

22. If your answer to Question 20 is YES, please circle the number in each of the columns "a" to "c". (Please add all the choices you made above, in case of multiple times of borrowing.)

	a. Banks	b. Microfinance institutions/ Microcredit organizations	c. Credit Unions
Yes, but only once	1	4	7
Yes, repeatedly	2	5	8
No	3	6	9

23. If your answer is YES, are you generally satisfied with the financial product you have taken and its accompanying services? (Single answer)

1. Yes
2. No (Please specify reasons: _____)

24. Would you be interested to take any financial product (e.g. loans) to fund any of the activities listed below <u>in the future</u>?

<u>If you are interested in none of the below activities, please proceed to Question 27.</u> (multiple choice)

1. Production of energy from renewable sources (e.g. solar panels, biogas plants)	Y/N
2. Electricity/heat/energy saving and management (e.g. house insulation, more efficient boilers)	Y/N
3. Management of water-use (e.g. more efficient irrigation systems, better access to clean water, etc.)	Y/N
4. Wastewater management	Y/N
5. Waste management	Y/N
6. Switching crops to the ones that are more environmentally-friendly or resilient to changing climate/weather	Y/N
7. Switching choice of livestock species and breeds	Y/N
8. Use of new and alternative feed crop varieties for livestock	Y/N
9. Protection of biodiversity and landscapes	Y/N
10. Management of forest resources (e.g. agro-forestry, wildfire reduction, etc.)	Y/N
11. Protection of ambient air (avoiding outdoor air pollution)	Y/N
12.Agriculture insurance or any other disaster risk insurance	Y/N
13. Any other activity (Please specify what the activity is.) _____	Y/N
14. Don't know	Y
15. No response	Y

25. If your answer to Question 24 is YES, what would be the average amount <u>per loan/product</u> you would be interested to take? (Even if you want to take multiple loans or other financial products, please indicate the amount on average per loan/product.) (Single answer)

  1. Up to USD 500 (Up to KGS 35 000)
  2. USD 501 to USD 1 000 (KGS 35 001 to KGS 70 000)
  3. USD 1 001 to USD 2 000 (KGS 70 001 to KGS 140 000)
  4. USD 2 001 to USD 5 000 (KGS 140 001 to KGS 350 000)
  5. USD 5 001 to USD 10 000 (KGS 350 001 to KGS 700 000)
  6. USD 10 001 to USD 50 000 (KGS 700 001 to KGS 3 500 000)
  7. More than USD 50 000 (More than KGS 3 500 000)
  8. Don't know
  9. No response

26. If your answer to Question 24 is YES, what barriers do you think you might face in actually taking such a loan/financial product? (Multiple choice)

  1. You do not have a bank account.
  2. You have difficulties in understanding how to access and use the banking services.
  3. Interest rate may be too high.
  4. Lending term may be too short.
  5. Repayment schedule may not be convenient enough.
  6. You may not have sufficient collateral to pledge.
  7. You may not have enough information about financial products to make a good decision.
  8. You may not have enough information about activities for which the funding should be used.
  9. You would be afraid of integrity issues such as corruption and bribes.
  10. Other barriers (Please specify)_____
  11. Don't know

12. No response

Please skip to Question 27.

27. If your answer to Question 24 is NO, why are you not interested in such a loan/financial product? (Multiple choice)

1. You will use your own funding (e.g. savings) and it is enough, hence will not take loans.
2. You do not have sufficient information about such loans or financial products to make a decision.
3. You think such loans or financial products would be too expensive for you.
4. You do not have enough information about activities for which the funding may be used.
5. Necessary equipment for the activities seems too expensive or unavailable in the Kyrgyz market.
6. Environmental regulations are not strict enough to incentivize you to take any actions listed in Question 24, hence you have no financial need.
7. You have other priorities and cannot use your credit for the activities listed in Question 24.
8. You are not interested in environmental protection or sustainable development in the first place.
9. Other reasons (Please specify.)_____

28. What kind of support would you like to receive to consider using financial products for any of the activities listed in Question 24? (Please choose the three most important ones for you).

1. Support to lower interest rates
2. Longer lending terms
3. Setting a grace period
4. Support for fulfilling collateral requirements
5. Further information about available financial products
6. Further information about technical solutions to be financed
7. Stricter environmental regulations
8. Other types of support (Please specify)_____

We thank you for your assistance in completing this form. It is important for us to know what you think and what your needs are. The form is completely anonymous.

If you have any feedback or comments, please indicate below.

Annex D. Survey questionnaire in Kyrgyz

Респондент тууралуу негизги маалымат

1. Респонденттин жынысы:

    1. Эркек

    2. Аял

2. Респонденттин жаш курагы (Жазыныз: _____жаш)

    1. 1. 18-20

    2. 2. 21-25

    3. 3. 26-35

    4. 4. 36-45

    5. 5. 46-55

    6. 6. 56-64

    7. 7. 65 жана андан улуу

3. Сиздин билимиңиз?

билими жок	1	колледж	7
башталгыч билим	2	бутпөгөн жогорку	8
бутпөгөн орто	3	1.	9
жалпы орто	4	илимий даража (кандидат, илимий доктор)	10
1.	5	(окубаңыз) билбейм	98
2.	6	(окубаңыз) жооптон баш тартуу	99

4. Сиздин үй-бүлөлүк статусуңуз кандай?

    1. Жалгыз бой, балдары жок

    2. Жалгыз бой, балдары бар

    3. Үйлөнгөн/турмушка чыккан, балдары жок

    4. Үйлөнгөн/турмушка чыккан, балдары бар

5. Сиздин үй-бүлөнүздүн орточо айлык кирешеси кандай (сом менен эсептегенде)? бүт кирешени эске алыңыз, айлык акы, пенсия, пособиелерди кошо эсептегенде. инт.: q5 *карточканы көрсөтүңүз*

700 сомго чейин	1	6001-8000 сом	9
701-900 сом	2	8001-10000 сом	10
901-1200 сом	3	10001-12000 сом	11
1201- 1500 сом	4	12001-15000 сом	12
1501-2000 сом	5	15001-18000 сом	13
2001-3000 сом	6	18001-20000 сом	14
3001-4000 сом	7	20001 сомдон ашык	15
4001-6000 сом	8	билбейм/ жооптон баш тартуу	99

6. Сизди кошо эсептегенде, үй-чарбаныздда канча адам жашайт? __/ __/(числосун жазыңыз)_____

7. Азыркы учурда сиз иштейсизби?

ооба	1	q9 суроого өтүңүз
жок	2	q8 суроосун сураңыз! жана анан q12 өтүңүз
(окубаңыз) билбейм	98	
(окубаңыз) жооп жок	99	

8. Эгерде сиз иштебесеңиз, сиздин статусуңуз кандай?

окуучу/студент	1	жумушсуз; жумуш издеген жокмун	5
пенсионер (жаш-курагы, оорусу)	2	башкасы (жазыңыз)_____	6
үй кызматында/ бала багуу – декреттик отпуск	3	(окубаңыз)билбейм	98
убактылуу жумушсуз; жумуш издейм	4	(окубаңыз) жооп жок	99

Эгерде q8-суроосуна жооп берсе, q12 өтүңүз!

9. Сиз кайсы сектордо иштейсиз – менчик, мамлекеттик же мамлекеттик эмес уюм (НПО)?

менчик	1	мамлекеттик эмес уюм (НПО)	3
мамлекеттик	2	(окубаңыз) билбейм/жооп жок	99

10. Сиздин азыркы жумушуңуз/ кызматыңыз кандай?

жетекчи, директор, директордун орун басары, менеджер	1	квалификациясы жок жумушчу	7
адис	2	дыйкан	8
техник, мастер	3	аскер кызматкери	9
ишканадагы кызматчы	4	башкасы (жазыңыз)	10
тейлөө чөйрөсүнүн кызматкери, соодагер	5	_____ билбейм/жооп жок	99
билимдүү жумушчу, уста	6		

11. Экономикалык активдүүлүктүн кайсы түрү Сиздин ишмердүүлүгүнүздүн чөйрөсүн баарынан жакшы көрсөтөт? (Бир жооп)

1. Өсүмдүк өстүрүүчүлүк (мис., пахта, тамеки, арпа, кант кызылчасы, беде уруктары, үрөндүк картошка)

2. Жемиштер жана жашылчалар (мис., помидор, бадыраң, томат-черри, жемиштер, алча, жаш буурчактар, дары чөптөр)

3. Мал чарбачылык (мис.,ири мүйүздүү малдарды багуу, эчкилер жана кой чарбачылыгы)

4. Куштун этин жана жумуртка өндүрүү

5. Багбанчылык

6. Айыл чарба продуктыларын кайра иштетүү

7. Текстиль

8. Майда машине куруу

9. Өнөр жайдын кайра иштетүүчү башка түрлөрү

10. Тоо кен казуу өнөр жайы жана кен казууларды иштеп чыгуу

11. Соода, транспорт, сактоо жана дүң соода

12. Чекене соода

13. Коммуналдык чөйрө (мисалга, энергия, суу, жылытуу)

14. Каржы жана камсыздандыруу

15. Кызмат көрсөтүүнүн башка тармактары

16. Мамлекеттик кызматкер же муниципалдык жумушчу (мис., айыл өкмөтү)

17. Илимий изилдөөлөр

18. Аскер кызматы

19. Жумушсуздук

20. Жооп жок

12. Калк жашаган жердеги элдин саны:

1. 1 миллион жана андан көп жашоочу

2. 500 000-999 9999 жашоочу

3. 100 000-499 999 жашоочу

4. 50 000-99 999 жашоочу

5. 10 000-49 999 жашоочу

6. 2 000-9 999 жашоочу

7. 2000ден аз жашоочу

13. Респондент ... жашайт (РЕСПОНДЕНТ ЖАШАГАН ОБЛАСТТЫ, БЕЛГИЛЕП КОЮҢУЗ)

	ОДИН ОТВЕТ:
Бишкек	1
Чүй	2
Талас	3
Нарын	4
Ысык-Көл	5
Ош шаары	6
Ош областы	7
Жалал -Абад областы	8
Баткен областы	9

Негизги тема боюнча суроолор

14. Сиздин банкта эсебиңиз барбы?

Ооба	1	Q15ке өтүңүз
Жок	2	Q16га өтүңүз
Билбейм	98	
Жооп жок	99	

15. Сиз мобилдик банкингди колдоносузбу?

Ооба	1
Жок	2
Билбейм	98
Жооп жок	99

16. Акыркы 5 жылда сиз кандай максатта болсо да, банктан же банктык эмес каржылык-кредиттик уюмдардан (микро кредиттик компаниялар, микро кредиттик агенттиктер, микро финансылык уюмдар, кредиттик союздар) кредит же финансылык продуктынын башка бир формасын алдыңыз беле? (Сураныч, «а»дан «с»га чейинки колонкалардын ар биринен номерди тегеректеп коюңуз).

	a. Банктар	b. Микрофинансылык уюмдар/ Микрокредиттик компаниялар/ Микрокредиттик агенттиктер	c. Кредиттик союздар
Ооба, бирок бир гана жолу	1	4	7
Ооба, бир нече жолу	2	5	8
Жок	3	6	9

17. Эгерде 16-суроого сиздин жообуңуз «ООБА»болсо, Сиз канча суммадагы акча алдыңыз эле? (Эгерде Сиз бир нече кредиттерди же башка финансылык продуктыларды алган болсоңуз, анда кредиттин/продуктынын орточо суммасын аныктаңыз) (Бир жооп) Эгерде 16-суроого сиздин жообуңуз «ЖОК»болсо, анда 19-суроого өтүңүз.

1. АКШ 500 долларга чейин   (35 000 сомго чейин)
2. АКШ 501 -1000 доллары   (35 001-70 000 сом)
3. АКШ 1 001 - 2 000 доллары   (70 001 - 140 000 сом)
4. АКШ 2 001 - 5 000 доллары   (140 001 - 350 000 сом)
5. АКШ 5 001 - 10 000 доллары (350 001 - 700 000 сом)
6. АКШ 10 001 - 50 000 доллары (700 001 - 3 500 000 сом)
7. АКШ 50 000 долларынан көп (3 500 000 сомдон көп)
8. Билбейм
9. Жооп жок

18. Эгерде 16-суроого сиздин жообуңуз «ООБА»болсо,   акча алууда сиздин негизги максатыңыз (максаттарыңыз) эмне болгон? (Бир нече варианттын болушу мүмкүн)

   1. Жеке (ипотека / турак жай)
   2. Жеке (башка максаттар)
   3. Бизнес (Негизги капиталга инвестициялар, мисалы, машиналар, объектилер, имараттар ж.б.)
   4. Бизнес (уруктар, эмгек акы төлөө, продукция үчүн чийки заттар ж.б. сыяктуу операциялык чыгымдар.)
   5. Карыздарды кайтаруу
   6. Билбейм
   7. Жооп жок

19. Эгерде 16-суроого сиздин жообуңуз «ЖОК» болсо,   анын негизги себеби (себептери) кандай? (Бир нече варианттын болушу мүмкүн)

   1. 1. Сиздин банктык эсебиңиз жок.
   2. 2. Сиздин банктык кызматтарды пайдалануу жана анын жолдорун түшүнүүгө кыйынчылыктарыңыз бар.
   3. 3. Кредит боюнча пайызы өтө жогору
   4. 4. Кредиттин мөөнөтү өтө эле кыска
   5. 5. Карыздарды жабуу графиги анча ыңгайлуу эмес
   6. 6. Сиздин күрөөгө коюуга каражатыңыз жетишсиз
   7. 7. Жакшы чечим кабыл алуу үчүн финансылык продуктылар жөнүндө жетиштүү маалыматыңыз жок
   8. 8.Бул каражаттарды пайдаланууга татыктуу болгон ишкердүүлүктүн түрү боюнча сизде жетиштүү маалымат жок
   9. 9. Ак ниеттүүлүккө байланышкан, жемкорук же пара алуу сыяктуу проблемалардан корктом.
   10. 10. Бардык башка себептер (сураныч, тактаңыз)_____
   11. 11. Билбейм
   12. 12. Жооп жок

20. [Эгерде 16-суроого сиздин жообуңуз «ООБА» болсо, анда бул суроого жооп бериңиз]. Акыркы 5 жылда сиз банктан же банктык эмес институттан төмөндөгү ишмердүүлүктүн бир түрү үчүн жабдууларды алууга кредиттерди же финансылык продуктынын башка бир формасын алдыңыз беле? (Бир нече жооптун болушу мүмкүн)

1. Кайра жанма булактардан энергия өндүрүү (мисалга, күн панелдери, биогаздык орнотмолор)	Ооба/Жок
2. Энергияны үнөмдөө (электр энергиясы, жылуулук энергиясы) жана электричествону/ жылуулук энергиясын башкаруу максатында (мисалы, үйдү изоляциялоо, кыйла натыйжалуу бойлерлер)	Ооба/Жок
3. Сууну колдонууну жөнгө салуу (мисалга, кыйла натыйжалуу сугаруу системалары, иче турган таза сууга мүмкүн болгон мыкты жол ж.б.)	Ооба/Жок
4. Агып чыккан сууларды башкаруу	Ооба/Жок
5. Таштандыларды башкаруу	Ооба/Жок
6. Кыйла экологиялык же климаттын/аба ырайынын өзгөрүүсүнө кыйла туруктуу болгон өсүмдүк өстүрүүгө өтүү	Ооба/Жок
7. Малды жана тукумун тандоодогу өзгөрүүлөр	Ооба/Жок
8. Мал чарбачылыгы үчүн тоют өсүмдүктөрүнүн жаңы жана атаандаш түрлөрүн колдонуу	Ооба/Жок
9. Биоартүрдүүлүгүн жана ландшафттарды коргоо	Ооба/Жок
10. Токой ресурстарын башкаруу (мис., агро токой чарбачылыгы, токой өрттөрүн кыскартуу ж.б.)	Ооба/Жок
11. Айлана-чөйрөдөгү абаны коргоо (атмосфералык абанын булганышын алдын алуу)	Ооба/Жок
12. Айыл чарбасын камсыздандыруу же табият кырсыктарынын бардык тобокелдигинен камсыздандыруу	Ооба/Жок
13. Бардык баша ишмердүүлүк (сураныч, ишмердүүлүктүн түрүн тактаңыз) _____	Ооба/Жок
14. Билбейм	Ооба
15. Жооп жок	Ооба

21. Эгерде 20-суроого Сиздин жообуңуз «ООБА» болсо, Сиз канча суммадагы акча алдыңыз эле? (Эгерде Сиз бир нече кредиттерди же башка финансылык продуктыларды алган болсоңуз, анда кредиттин/продуктынын орточо суммасын аныктаңыз) (Бир жооп)

    1. АКШ 500 долларга чейин   (35 000 сомго чейин)

    2. АКШ 501 -1000 доллары   (35 001-70 000 сом)

    3. АКШ 1 001 - 2 000 доллары   (70 001 - 140 000 сом)

    4. АКШ 2 001 - 5 000 доллары   (140 001 - 350 000 сом)

    5. АКШ 5 001 - 10 000 доллары   (350 001 - 700 000 сом)

    6. АКШ 10 001 - 50 000 доллары (700 001 - 3 500 000 сом)

    7. АКШ 50 000 долларынан көп (3 500 000 сомдон көп)

    8. Билбейм

    9. Жооп жок

22. Эгерде 20-суроого Сиздин жообуңуз «ООБА» болсо,   «а»дан «с»га чейинки колонкалардын ар биринен номерди тегеректеп коюңуз. (Сураныч, Эгерде Сиз бир нече жолу кредиттерди алган болсоңуз, Сиз жогоруда тандаган бардык варианттарды кошуңуз)

	a. Банктар	b. Микрофинансылык уюмдар/ Микрокредиттик компаниялар/ Микрокредиттик агенттиктер	c. Кредиттик союздар
Ооба, бирок бир гана жолу	1	4	7
Ооба, бир нече жолу	2	5	8
Жок	3	6	9

23. Эгерде 20-суроого Сиздин жообуңуз «ООБА» болсо, айтыңызчы, Сиз алган финансылык продуктыларга жана аны коштогон кызмат көрсөтүүлөргө негизинен ыраазысызбы? (Бир жооп)

    1. Ооба

    2. Жок (сураныч, себебин тактаңыз: _____)

24. Келечекте, төмөндөгү аталган ишмердүүлүктүн кайсы түрүн болсо да каржылоо үчүн кандайдыр бир финансылык продукт алуу (мис., кредиттер) Сиз үчүн кызыктуу болот

76 |

beле? Эгерде Сизге төмөндө аталган ишмердүүлүктүн түрлөрүнүн бири да Сизге кызыксыз болсо, 27-суроого өтүңүз. (Бир нече варианттар болушу мүмкүн)

1. Кайра жанма булактардан энергия өндүрүү (мисалга, күн панелдери, биогаздык орнотмолор)	Ооба/Жок
2. Энергияны үнөмдөө (электр энергиясы, жылуулук энергиясы) жана электричествону/ жылуулук энергиясын башкаруу максатында (мисалы, үйдү изоляциялоо, кыйла натыйжалуу бойлерлер)	Ооба/Жок
3. Сууну колдонууну жөнгө салуу (мисалга, кыйла натыйжалуу сугаруу системалары, иче турган таза сууга мүмкүн болгон мыкты жол ж.б.)	Ооба/Жок
4. Агып чыккан сууларды башкаруу	Ооба/Жок
5. Таштандыларды башкаруу	Ооба/Жок
6. Кыйла экологиялык же климаттын/аба ырайынын өзгөрүүсүнө кыйла туруктуу болгон өсүмдүк өстүрүүгө өтүү	Ооба/Жок
7. Малды жана тукумун тандоодогу өзгөрүүлөр	Ооба/Жок
8. Мал чарбачылыгы үчүн тоют өсүмдүктөрүнүн жаңы жана атаандаш түрлөрүн колдонуу	Ооба/Жок
9. Биоартүрдүүлүгүн жана ландшафттарды коргоо	Ооба/Жок
10. Токой ресурстарын башкаруу (мис., агро токой чарбачылыгы, токой өрттөрүн кыскартуу ж.б.)	Ооба/Жок
11. Айлана-чөйрөдөгү абаны коргоо (атмосфералык абанын булганышын алдын алуу)	Ооба/Жок
12. Айыл чарбасын камсыздандыруу же табият кырсыктарынын бардык тобокелдигинен камсыздандыруу	Ооба/Жок
13. Бардык баша ишмердүүлүк (сураныч, ишмердүүлүктүн түрүн тактаңыз) _____	Ооба/Жок
14. Билбейм	Ооба
15. Жооп жок	Ооба

25. Эгерде 24-суроого Сиздин жообуңуз «ООБА» болсо, сиз кызыккан кредиттердин/продуктынын орточо суммасы канча болот эле? (Эгерде Сиз бир нече кредит же башка финансылык продуктыларды алгыңыз келсе да, сураныч, орточо 1 кредитке карата суммасын аныктаңыз) (Бир жооп)

1. АКШ 500 долларга чейин (35 000 сомго чейин)
2. АКШ 501 -1000 доллары (35 001-70 000 сом)
3. АКШ 1 001 - 2 000 доллары (70 001 - 140 000 сом)
4. АКШ 2 001 - 5 000 доллары (140 001 - 350 000 сом)
5. АКШ 5 001 - 10 000 доллары (350 001 - 700 000 сом)
6. АКШ 10 001 - 50 000 доллары (700 001 - 3 500 000 сом)
7. АКШ 50 000 долларынан көп (3 500 000 сомдон көп)
8. Билбейм
9. Жооп жок

26. Эгерде 24-суроого Сиздин жообуңуз «ООБА» болсо, эгерде сиз чынында эле мындай кредитти/финансылык продуктыны алууну чечсеңиз, сиз кандай тоскоолдуктарга туш болмокмун деп ойлойсуз? (Бир нече варианттар болушу мүмкүн)

1. Сиздин банктык эсебиңиз жок.
2. Сизде банктык кызматтарды пайдалануу жана анын жолдорун түшүнүүгө кыйынчылыктарыңыз бар.
3. Кредит боюнча пайызы өтө жогору
4. Кредиттин мөөнөтү өтө эле кыска
5. Карыздарды жабуу графиги анча ыңгайлуу эмес
6. Сиздин күрөөгө коюуга каражатыңыз жетишсиз
7. Жакшы чечим кабыл алуу үчүн финансылык продуктылар жөнүндө жетиштүү маалыматыңыз жок
8. Бул каражаттарды пайдаланууга татыктуу болгон ишкердүүлүктүн түрү боюнча сизде жетиштүү маалымат жок

ACCESSING AND USING GREEN FINANCE IN THE KYRGYZ REPUBLIC © OECD 2021

9. Ак ниеттүүлүккө байланышкан, жемкорук же пара алуу сыяктуу проблемалардан корком.

10. Бардык башка себептер (сураныч, тактаңыз)_____

11. Билбейм

12. Жооп жок

ИНТ: Сураныч, 28-суроого өтүңүз.

27. Эгерде 24-суроого Сиздин жообуңуз «ЖОК» болсо, Сиз эмне үчүн кредитке/финансылык продуктылар сыяктууларга кызыкпайсыз? (Бир нече варианттар болушу мүмкүн)

1. Сиз өзүңүздүн менчик каражаттарыңызды пайдаланасыз (мисалга, чогулткан акча) жана ал жетиштүү, ошондуктан кредиттерди албайсыз

2. Чечимдерди кабыл алуу үчүн сиздин мындай кредиттер же финансылык продуктылар жөнүндө жетиштүү маалыматыңыз жок.

3. Сиз мындай кредиттер же финансылык продуктылар Сиз үчүн абдан кымбатка турат деп ойлойсуз.

4. Бул каражаттарды пайдалануу үчүн ишмердүүлүктүн түрлөрү жөнүндө Сиздин жетиштүү маалыматыңыз жок

5. Ишмердүүлүктүн мындай түрлөрү үчүн зарыл болгон жабдуулар өтө эле кымбат көрүнөт же болбосо, Кыргызстандын рыногунда бул мүмкүн эмес

6. 24-суроодо аталган кандайдыр бир иш аракеттерди жасоого Сизди кызыктыруу үчүн экологиялык нормалар кыйла катаал, Сиздин эч кандай финансылык зарылдыгыңыз жок.

7. Сиздин башка артыкчылыктарыңыз бар жана 24-суроодо көрсөтүлгөн иш-аракеттерге Сиз өзүңүздүн кредитиңизди колдоно албайсыз.

8. Сиз айлана-чөйрөнү коргоого же биринчи кезекте туруктуу өнүгүүгө кызыкпайсыз

9. Башка себептер (Сураныч, көрсөтүңүз.)_____

28. 24-суроодо аталган кандайдыр бир иш-аракеттер үчүн финансылык продуктыларды пайдаланууну караштыруу үчүн Сиз колдоонун кандай түрүн алгыңыз келет? (Сураныч, Сиз үчүн баарынан маанилүү болгон үчөөнү тандаңыз)

1. Пайыздык ставканы төмөндөтүү боюнча колдоо

2. Кредиттин мөөнөтүнүн кыйла узактыгы

3. Жеңилдик берүү мезгилин белгилөө

4. Күрөө менен камсыз кылуу талаптарын аткаруу үчүн колдоо

5. Мүмкүн болгон финансылык продуктылар жөнүндөгү мындан аркы маалыматтар

6. Каржылоо мүмкүн болгон техникалык чечимдер жөнүндө мындан аркы маалыматтар

7. Кыйла катаал экологиялык нормалар

8. Колдоонун башка түрү (Сураныч, тактаңыз)_____

Бул форманы толтурууга кошкон Сиздин жардамыңыз үчүн Сизге ыраазычылык билдиребиз. Сиздин эмне деп ойлогонуңуз жана Сиздин кандай муктаждыктарыңызды билүү биз үчүн маанилүү. Бул форма толугу менен жашыруун.

Эгерде сиздин пикириңиз же комментарийлериңиз болсо, аны төмөн жакка жазыңыз.